Godless
for God's Sake

Nontheism in Contemporary Quakerism

by 27 Quaker Nontheists
Edited by David Boulton

Dales Historical Monographs
Hobsons Farm, Dent, Cumbria LA10 5RF, UK

Published by
Dales Historical Monographs
Hobsons Farm, Dent, Cumbria LA10 5RF, UK
Tel: 015396 25321
davidboulton1@compuserve.com

ISBN 0-9511578-6-8

Printed by
Stramongate Press, Aynam Mills, Little Aynam, Kendal,
Cumbria LA9 7AH

This book is printed on recycled paper

First Printing February 2006
Second Printing July 2006
Third Printing July 2007

Front cover: *Geraniums and Nipplewort,*
Gouache, by John Cooke, The Studio, Dent, Cumbria, England.
Reproduced by kind permission of the artist.

"Man's last and highest parting occurs when, for God's sake, he takes leave of God".

- Meister Eckhart (13th century)

Contents

11. This is my Story, This is my Song …

In the Beginning ...

This collection of essays began as a gleam in the eye during a workshop for nontheist Quakers at Woodbrooke Quaker Study Centre, Birmingham, England, in 2004. The gleam became a firm intent at Pendle Hill Quaker Center, Philadelphia, in May 2005. The Center's first event for nontheist Friends had just concluded. Spirits were high. Os Cresson, Robin Alpern and I met for lunch and pondered "what next?". In the United States, Os and Robin (and her father before her) have been quietly making a case for the inclusion of nontheists in the Quaker family for many years. In Britain, I have publicly advocated a Quaker humanism since the 1980s. A book like this seemed long overdue.

What we have put together is ten essays followed by a collection of short "testimonies". The essays demonstrate the rich variety of nontheist Quaker experience: there is no uniform bloc or faction at work! Some are directly experiential, some more theoretical, one or two historical, and one is a statistical survey. Six are from American Friends, two from British, one from an Australian, and one is an Anglo-American co-production.

The inspiring collection of 19 shorter experiential pieces and testimonies that concludes the book under the only slightly tongue-in-cheek title "This is my story, this is my song" contains 13 contributions from the USA, five from Britain and one from New Zealand. The writers' ages range from 18 to 80-plus. Readers may consider sampling this closing chapter first, before moving on to the longer essays.

The majority of our contributors - 27 all told, from four countries and no fewer than thirteen Yearly Meetings (listed below) - are Friends of many years standing and hold or have held office in their local, monthly or yearly meetings. These are not a new breed of entryists, invading a Society the religious and Christian roots of which they do not understand or appreciate!

Many simply ask for nothing more than acceptance of nontheism as part of the diversity of modern liberal and creedless Quakerism. Some hope to see a nontheistic understanding of human spirituality gradually replace traditional theism, not only in the Religious Society of Friends but in the wider Christian church and other faith communities as together they face up to the daunting challenges of the 21st century - challenges to which supernaturalism seems irrelevant.

But theist or nontheist, we share the Quaker tradition, Quaker worship, Quaker language. Together we understand Quakerism as a way rather than a doctrine. If this little book contributes to a deeper understanding of the breadth and diversity of our radical tradition, the varieties of our experience of worship and the richness of possibilities inherent in our Quaker language, it will serve a useful purpose.

And because the Religious Society of Friends is only one among many Christian-rooted denominations, and Christianity itself is only one colour in the rainbow spectrum of religious and humanist traditions, we hope this book will be read by many who may have no prior knowledgeof the Quaker tradition but find that a nontheist and non-supernaturalist spirituality speaks to their condition.

For such non-Quaker readers, it may be useful to mention that the Religious Society of Friends (Quakers) originated in 17th century Britain in the heat of the English revolution and has no creed or compulsory belief system, no professional priests or clerics (though some American branches have pastors), no infallible scripture, and no spiritual elite determining what is and what is not "sound doctrine". The Society is defined by its values and "testimonies" rather than by dogma. Friends are a diverse lot - but they are, first and foremost, friends.

★★★

Observant readers will note a number of stylistic inconsistencies in the essays that follow. With contributors from both sides of the Atlantic, and two from the far side of the Pacific, the editor has had to deal with not one English language but at least two, and perhaps four. So I have left the Americans to the spellings they favor and the British (and Commonwealth) contributors to those they favour. I have meddled a little more adventurously with a bewilderingly varied use of punctuation, but in this as in my other editorial duties I have tried to do so with a light touch, which means turning a blind eye to minor inconsistencies.

I am grateful to all contributors and the wider groups of nontheist Friends who have helped put the book together. Special thanks must go to Os

Cresson who assisted me in more ways than I have space to enumerate, but particularly in putting together the final chapter, and in helping me access the variety of formats in which the essays made their mysterious journey through cyber-space. Any remaining textual errors, however, are my responsibility, for which I apologise to writers and readers alike.

David Boulton
Dent, Cumbria, UK
January 2006

Contributors come from the following Yearly Meetings:

Aotearoa/New Zealand (1)
Australia (1)
Baltimore, USA (2)
Britain (7)
Iowa Conservative, USA (1)
Lake Erie, USA (1)
New England, USA (4)
New York, USA (3)
Northern, USA (1)
Pacific, USA (1)
Philadelphia, USA (3)
Southern Appalachian, USA (1)
Unaffiliated, USA (1)

For God's Sake? An Introduction

David Boulton

Zounds! I was never so bethumped with words!
- William Shakespeare, 'King John'.

Godless for God's Sake will seem to some a provocative, even shocking, title for a book by Quakers whose authors boldly hope to reach a readership both in the world-wide Religious Society of Friends and other Christian, post-Christian and liberal religious communities. In what sense would members of a movement which only a few generations back was proud to call itself "the harmless people of God called Quakers" wish to describe themselves as "Godless"? And why "for God's sake"?

As if this were not paradox enough, there's that word *nontheism* in the sub-title. Is not Quakerism a Christian denomination? Is it not a *Religious* Society of Friends? Even if it now includes members and attenders who prefer not to call themselves Christians, is it not abundantly clear that the Society's historical roots are deeply embedded in the Protestant Christian tradition? And is not this tradition, however varied its expressions, essentially a *theist* tradition - one that has "God", "the Spirit", "the divine" at the core of its language, its faith and its practice? What is a *nontheist* but an *atheist*, and what place can there be for the atheist, the unbeliever, in a professedly religious Society?

Good, reasonable questions. This book is an attempt - or rather a collection of attempts - to offer answers. The plural is important. There is no one answer, no unified or official "nontheist Quaker view" - any more than there is one official theist Quaker view. Each writer in this collection speaks his or her own truth, and these truths, known experimentally (that is, through personal experience), are no less diverse than the well-recognised diversity of theistic traditions. None of us speak for all Quaker nontheists, any more than any Friend, theist or nontheist, may claim to speak for all Quakers. And that goes for this introductory editorial chapter no less than for those that follow.

First, then, the title of our little book. *Godless for God's Sake* is suggested by the famous passage in Sermon 23 by the mediaeval mystic Meister Eckhart: "Man's last and highest parting occurs when, for God's sake, he takes leave of God". What Eckhart meant by "taking leave of God" was argued over by his readers, by the ecclesiastical judges in his heresy trial, and by his many and varied followers. A modern interpreter, Raymond Bernard Blakney (*Meister Eckhart: a Modern Translation*), suggests that Eckhart was keen to distinguish between what we might wish to be true and what we find to be true experimentally. "What Eckhart demands is equivalent to what pure science demands of the laboratory investigator. He means to say that the price of truth is self-denial in things spiritual, as well as in things material and intellectual."

It is in this most demanding sense that we describe ourselves as Godless for God's sake, taking leave of an idol for the sake of the values and the truth the idol has been held to represent. It is in this sense, too, that Don Cupitt, in his 1979 classic *Taking Leave of God*, launched a modern Christian nontheism which found its theological expression in what he called "nonrealism", and its organisational expression in the Sea of Faith Networks in Britain, Australia and New Zealand.

But what of this word *nontheism*? It does not appear in the standard dictionaries alongside other negative words like "non-existence" (first used in 1648) and "nonsensical" (1655). But *theism* is there. The Oxford English Dictionary gives it two distinct meanings. We may ignore the 1886 one - "a morbid condition characterized by headache, sleeplessness, and palpitation of the heart, caused by excessive tea-drinking" - and note the one traced back to 1678: "Belief in a deity or deities... Belief in the existence of God... especially belief in one God as creator and supreme ruler of the universe".

Nontheism, then, is the opposite: the absence of any belief in a deity or deities, in the existence of God (where "existence" is understood in a realist, objective sense), and especially belief in one God as creator and supreme ruler. What then distinguishes nontheism from atheism, particularly as the OED defines atheism (1587) as "disbelief in, or denial of, the existence of a God", and "practical atheism" as "godlessness"?

Labels are nearly always problematic. Publication of this book was preceded by lively discussion among its principal contributors of what label best describes a Quaker (or a member of any other religious body) who does not believe in the existence of a deity or deities. Some were happy to be labelled "atheists" as the simplest and most straightforward way of signifying their position, ready to accept the opprobrium that so often comes with the word. Others, however, rejected the term because of the implication it has acquired of militant opposition to all forms of religious expression and practice. Some preferred "agnostic", Thomas Huxley's coinage for one who holds that the existence of God, or anything beyond material phenomena, cannot be known. Others rejected this, again for what has become the popular usage of the word as signifying those who can't make up their mind one way or the other. Some liked "naturalist", to distinguish their position from that of supernaturalists. Others objected that this might be misunderstood as a penchant for bird-watching or nudism. Some wanted to rescue "humanist" from the wholly secular and anti-religious connotations it came to acquire in the late twentieth century: at least, they argued, it is a positive term, a *pro*-word rather than a *non*-word. But others objected that a human-centred stance denied the indivisibility of life and "creation".

So, in the absence of agreement on atheist, agnostic, naturalist or humanist, we settled on nontheist. It is not perfect, not least because it defines us negatively as *non*-believers in this rather than positive believers in that. But *nontheist* has emerged as the least disliked option! We therefore use "Quaker nontheist" here as a general term embracing Quaker atheists, Quaker agnostics, Quaker naturalists and Quaker humanists: all who find that their own way of being valiant for truth is to declare themselves Godless - for God's sake.

Some will ask, Why have a label at all? Are not labels invariably divisive? Why not just "Quaker" or "Friend"? Those who ask these questions have evidently not noticed that Quaker and Friend are themselves labels (and seventeenth-century Christians found them intensely divisive!). Religious labels have the useful function of distinguishing one group from another, say Episcopalians and Seventh Day Adventists. That is the function of labels on jam pots: they usefully distinguish the strawberry from the raspberry. A grocery store that insisted on labelling them all "jam", without distinction, would cause unnecessary confusion and irritation. The purpose of labelling is the avoidance of confusion and the promotion of clarity: that is why we distinguish between conservative and liberal theologies, between programmed and unprogrammed meetings, between universalist and christocentric emphases. So it makes for sense and clarity to distinguish between theist and nontheist conceptual frameworks. Those who charge that this is unnecessarily divisive are often simply wishing that the distinctions were not there, or preferring that we pretend they don't exist. Far better, I suggest, to acknowledge our diversity, recognise it as a strength, celebrate it, explore it, and - for the sake of clarity and integrity - label it.

But it is not merely in the superficial process of labelling and sub-labelling that readers of these essays and of a wider Quaker nontheist literature will find considerable diversity of view. Some Quaker nontheists have wholly abandoned "God language" and hope for a progressive relinquishment of such language within the Society. Some choose not to use the word "God" themselves but are happy to "translate" it when it is used by other Friends in written or spoken ministry or in conversation. Some have no problem using traditional Quaker Godspeak - "God", "that of God", "the Spirit", "the divine", "the inner light" - understanding these hallowed and resonant terms metaphorically, symbolically, poetically, instrumentally, signifying the sum of our human values, the imagined embodiment of our human ideals, the focus of our ultimate concern: no more, but, gloriously, no less than all that makes up the wholly human spirit.

I should acknowledge here that nontheists are a minority within what has always been a predominantly theistic Society. But they are not an insignificant minority. The various surveys skilfully summarised by David Rush in Chapter 10 show that in 1989 some 26% of British Friends said they did not believe in God or were "not sure", and the percentage was virtually unchanged at 26.5 when the question was asked again in 2003. A survey of Philadelphia Yearly Meeting Friends, USA, in 2002 indicated that only 43.7% of the 552 members and attenders questioned said they believed in the traditional God who could be prayed to with the expectation of receiving an answer: 37.0% said they did not, and 19.0% said they had no definite belief either way. Even allowing for the notoriously slippery ambiguities of words like "God", "belief", "pray" and "answer", the numbers of "non-believers" is remarkably high: higher, as some have been quick to observe, than the number of non-believers in the population at large. And David Rush's own 2002 survey of 199 British and American Quaker nontheists indicated that the great majority of those who so describe themselves have been members of the Society for more than twenty years and have served as local meeting, Monthly Meeting, and even Yearly Meeting clerks. Nontheism clearly has an established place in the Religious Society of Friends.

★★★

But perhaps I am starting in the wrong place. This little essay and the essays it introduces reflect the concerns of one group of Friends on the fringes of a Society which is itself on the fringes of Christian nonconformity, which in turn is on the fringes of Protestantism, which is no more than a segment of the Christian tradition, which is only one colour in the rainbow of the world's historic religious cultures. We are, after all, small beer. That does not mean our concerns are of no value - there would be no point in labouring to produce this book if we believed that - but it does behove us, when we speak our truth, to do so with some awareness of the bigger picture, the wider religious context of the first decade of the third millennium of the Common Era.

That means recognising what has happened to religion in modern times. The 19th century saw Neitzsche's proclamation of the death of God, and Darwin's undermining of the notion that He had ever lived or been necessary in the first place. Marx dismissed religion as the opium of the people and Freud taught that God was just one more neurosis. Many Unitarians, who had already reduced God from three persons to one, decided even that was one too many and turned humanist. Secular humanists developed an ethic that bypassed God altogether and looked to a coming time when irrational religious faith would follow the old gods into the grave. And for a time it looked as if they'd got it right. Church attendance fell, slowly but surely in the USA, rapidly in Europe. In the developed world, at least, the same was true of religious observance generally. He and she that had ears to hear caught the "melancholy, long, withdrawing roar" of Matthew Arnold's out-going tide of the sea of faith "retreating, to the breath of the night-wind, down the vast edges drear and naked shingles of the world". Whether they mourned or celebrated the twilight of gods, devils and things that go bump in the night, a growing number of folk shared a sense that religion was yesterday's big yawn.

But tides turn. And when the tide of religion turned in the late twentieth century it came in with the destructive force of a tsunami. The sheer, bewildering complexity and insecurity of post-modern, post-industrial, post-war life lent to the old mysteries and metaphysics a sentimental, nostalgic glow. Old-time religion, "good enough for Moses" and for Grandpa, seemed once again "good enough for me" - especially when it came in new packaging. Churches in Britain continued to empty but the mind/body/spirit shelves in the bookshops groaned under the weight of tomes recommending a thousand varieties of bottled spirituality - three for the price of two. One in ten British men and one in four women tell pollsters they think there's something in reincarnation. One in three women say they believe in angels, especially the guardian variety. Over half the American population claim to be born-again, and their grotesque telly-evangelists run empires that stretch from Little Rock to Vladivostok. Africa is awash with mission-planted happy-clappy churchianity, including a Quaker variety. God is invoked by all sides in what, ironically, is still called by some "the Holy Land". George Bush and Osama bin Laden both claim God gives them their marching orders, and a century after free-thinkers organised God's funeral, monstrous and murderous religious fundamentalisms square up to each other, for God's sake and in his name, in a fight to the death.

There is little that is liberal, modern, progressive, rational, truthful, beautiful or loving about the tide of Christian, Islamic and Zionist bigotry which is turning half the world into Arnold's "darkling plain, swept with confused alarms of struggle and flight, where ignorant armies clash by night". Religion is no longer the ointment, the bandage, the *salve* of salvation: it is the raw wound, and the smell of gangrene fills the air.

It is at this point that the good and godly in our religious societies and our Religious Society say "Yes, but that's not because God is dead, but because people mis-use religion and commandeer God for their own wicked purposes". That men and women do just that is undeniable, as is the evident fact, also pointed out by believers, that unbelievers have not lagged behind in the bloody business of building their republics of hell on earth. But this defence of "*true* religion" raises the big question of how we distinguish the true from the false, the good from the bad. "By their fruits ye shall know them"? But who judges which fruit is ripe, refreshing and life-giving, and which is way past its sell-by date? By scripture? But whose scripture? By intuition? But what when your intuition and mine lead us in opposite directions? When George Bush and Osama bin Laden both claim to be hearing the voice of God and doing his will? When Quakers and suicide-bombers each claim to be following the leadings of the Spirit? And if that last question seems preposterous, consider the following prayer:

Oh God, open all doors for me. Oh God, who answers prayers and answers those who ask you, I am asking you for your help. I am asking you for forgiveness. I am asking you to lighten my way... God, I trust in you. God, I lay myself in your hands. I ask with the light of faith that has lit the whole world and lightened all darkness on earth, guide me!

It could be the prayer of an evangelical Christian or a liberal Quaker. It was in fact the prayer of Mohamed Atta, written on a scrap of paper found in his luggage after he had crashed his plane into the twin towers and thereby earned his passport to Paradise.

Surely what links Bush and bin Laden, church, synagogue and mosque, Bible and Koran, is the conviction that there is an Ultimate Authority in human affairs; that this Ultimate Authority is transcendent, super-human and absolute; that *our particular tradition* has either sole access to it, or at least is best able to interpret it; that this Ultimate Authority, Ultimate Truth, knows what is best for us; and that we obey or disobey it at our peril.

That's theism. And it is high time we recognised it for what it is: our problem, rather than our salvation.

★★★

So what am I suggesting? That religion is one long mistake, one big lie, one vast illusion? Hardly. We do not have to look far to find examples of the inspirational *salving-power* of the religious impulse: in our great art galleries and cathedrals, in our poetry and literature, our mythologies and music, our dance and drama: in Gandhi and Martin Luther King: in the Salvation Army soup kitchen, the Red Cross and the Red Crescent, the Jubilee campaign: and, yes, in Quaker Social Action. We need the religious impulse. What we don't need is its supernaturalist foundation. Why pin our human values of truth, beauty, integrity, compassion, to a fantasy realm, an other-world, the siren promises of an after-life, the notion that we are creatures of a supernatural, super-human being? Why, in poet Stevie Smith's piercing accusation, "allow good to be hitched to a lie"?

The "lie" is not God, but the simplistic, literalist notion of God: the notion that "he" or "she" or "it" exists independently of our human consciousness encoded in human language. What is so dangerous about such literalism is that it relieves us humans from final responsibility for the way we shape our destiny, promotes a paralysing fatalism, trivialises this life as mere preparation for a life to come, endows the "godly" with a spurious legitimacy and demonises the "ungodly".

But supernaturalism is not the only option. Religious humanists or nontheists, if they do not choose to jettison God-language altogether, may re-envision God without resort to such crude literalism. (And "re-envisioning God" is what we humans have been doing ever since we came up with the god-idea. The tribal monster-god of ancient Israel who had his mobile home in the ark of the covenant came to be re-envisioned as a transcendent heavenly father, who was in turn re-envisioned as the Word made flesh in Jesus, re-envisioned again by 17th century Friends as a God no less immanent than transcendent, an inner or inward light of conscience. We don't have to suppose the re-envisioning came to a sudden end in 1652.)

One way to re-envision God in the 21st century is to see him as the protagonist in our great heritage of God-stories. This God is our human creation, our imaginative fiction. As we made stories to make sense of our world, we built them around this central character, imagined in our own image. God - indeed, all the gods, spirits, angels, devils, demons - are our own literary creations. They are real in the sense that Shakespeare's Hamlet and Juliet, Homer's Odysseus, Sophocles' Antigone, Melville's Ahab and Mozart's Queen of the Night are real. And as these fictional protagonists represent *human* characteristics, typify *human* values and illuminate the *human* condition, so too does the God of the Bible. To bracket God with Hamlet and the rest will seem absurd or sacreligious only to those who do not understand the key role of story-telling in the construction of meaning. Shakespeare's fictional Hamlet is far more real and rounded, far more *human*, than the historical Amleth on whom he is supposedly based. Shakespeare's prince invested humanity with inwardness, introspection, by means of the new device of soliloquy, which is why critic Harold Bloom calls him the first of the moderns (and Shakespeare's work "the invention of the human"). Amleth lived, fought, died, and is no more. Hamlet will live for ever. That's what fiction at its most powerful and transcendent can do, and God as story surpasses all other fiction.

When we enter a new world by sitting in the darkness to see *A Midsummer Night's Dream* through a magical proscenium arch we do not protest that it is nonsense because science has shown that there are no fairies at the bottom of our garden, or anywhere else. When we read the books or watch the films of Tolkien's *The Lord of the Rings* we do not complain that science has produced no evidence for the existence of hobbits, ents and orcs. We know we are in the realms of the imagination. We know that through these imaginary fairies, hobbits, ents and orcs we are exploring and celebrating what it is to be human: what it means to be what we are, our light and our darkness, "the glory, jest, and riddle of the world" as Pope sums us up. And that is how it is, too, when we knowingly perform the same "suspension of disbelief" in the drama of religious worship, slipping out of our everyday prose into the poetry of God-language. Allowing good to be hitched to a fiction, an image, a symbol, is very different from hitching it to a lie.

But understanding God in this fictive and symbolic way has a further dimension. It requires us to think through what the word God is symbolising. What is the substance of the metaphor? What is it we are praising, affirming, celebrating, when we praise, affirm and celebrate God?

What else but the values our tradition has assigned to God?: truth, integrity, justice, compassion and loving kindness. Are not these precisely what the word God stands for?

The late first or early second century writer of John's gospel tells us what God means: God is love. The Sufi poets tell us "the light in our souls, that is God". The 17th century proto-Quaker Gerrard Winstanley (see Chapter 9) tells us God is reason, community, love. William Blake tells us "all deities reside in the human breast", and that God *is* "mercy, pity, peace and love": all human values.

For mercy has a human heart,
Pity a human face,
And love the human form divine
And peace a human dress.

The 19th century author of *The Essence of Christianity*, Ludwig Feuerbach, tells us that love "is God himself, and apart from it there is no God". Love in action provides the building blocks of faith. For Feuerbach, an atheist is one who denies not the objective *existence* of God but the *predicates* of God: love, compassion, wisdom, justice. One may *believe in* God in the sense of trusting these values to the point of according them ultimate authority. But that is quite different from *believing that* God himself, or herself, or itself, exists.

Illustration: An Indian doctor practising in London decorates his surgery with a splendid statue of Ganesh, the Hindu god with an elephant's face. One of his patients is a little taken aback, wondering how a sophisticated, well-educated physician can give room-space to so bizarre a deity. So he tackles the doctor: "Do you really believe in the existence of a god with an elephant's face?" And the doctor replies, "I believe, trust and have complete faith in every attribute of Ganesh - except his existence!"

The nontheist Quaker - at least, this nontheist Quaker - believes, trusts and has complete faith in the attributes of a God he understands to be no more, but gloriously no less, than the symbol of those values. I, for one, would no more eliminate God-language from our religious discourse than I would eliminate rhyme and rhythm from poetry. I do not wish to celebrate Blake's "virtues of delight" in the language of my local newspaper when there is a richer language available, one that reaches the parts everyday language cannot touch. So when, in Quaker business meetings, we seek the leadings of the Spirit, I do not suppose that we are awaiting instruction from the creator of the universe, or that we are in some kind of mystical communication with the holy ghost of Jesus. But I do believe that the wholly human spirit of "mercy, pity, peace and love" demands a hearing, and that we are unwise not to heed it.

★★★

None of this is particularly new, original or innovative. From the Enlightenment onward the old supernaturalism began to crack. That it has not only survived into modernity but even revived in postmodernity highlights our appetite for magic and mystery (or our addiction to superstition) and our extraordinary inability to distinguish wishful thinking from thinking. But it no longer holds the stage alone and unchallenged. The "radical reformation" of the mid-17th century, where Quakers were in the vanguard, began a process whereby God was gradually hauled down from the skies and put back where he belongs, in the human breast. From then on, the reaction and dogmatism of the Christian church began to be tempered by the civilising effects of liberal humanism (though the process still has a long way to go). Not only science but Biblical criticism, historical research and a renewed understanding of the function of myth and story produced a radically humanised theology. As Don Cupitt saw it in *Philosophy's Own Religion*, "The last stage in the historical evolution of religion is universal religious humanism, and the last ethic is humanitarianism".

The nineteenth and twentieth centuries saw religious humanism take a variety of forms, some within and some without the old institutions. Unitarianism, especially in its more vibrant American form, evolved into Unitarian Universalism. "Ethical societies" and humanist churches struggled for a toe-hold on hostile territory. A long line of distinguished theologian-philosophers introduced and defended such notions as "Religionless Christianity" and "the Gospel of Christian Atheism". In Britain, Australia and New Zealand, religious humanists, many from within the Anglican and mainstream nonconformist churches, came together in the Sea of Faith networks, their object being (in the words of the British network's constitution) to "explore and promote religious faith as a human creation". In America the Westar Institute in Santa Rosa, California, launched the Jesus Seminar and a broader campaign for "religious literacy" based on critical scholarship and evidence-based analysis. These are just a few of the many organisations exploring and promoting a humanistic Christianity.

Nor are these moves confined within the Christian tradition. A network of synagogues preaching and practising "Humanistic Judaism" has been established in the United States, and in Britain Stephen Bachelor's book *Buddhism Without Belief* has opened up a new humanistic Buddhism, shorn of ancient supernaturalisms. If religious humanism is still largely confined to the fringes, viewed with equal suspicion by the religious and secular establishments, it has nevertheless found a voice which, still and small against the universal cacophony of the religious market-place, cannot now be silenced.

How then do we amplify that voice? How do we build a new secular spirituality - *secular* in the root sense of being of this age and this world, and *spiritual* in the sense of affirming the non-material values which are the essence of the human spirit? What contribution can we make to the desupernaturalisation of religion, the marriage of reason and imagination, mind and heart combining to build a reasonable faith for the twenty-first century?

Where better to start than among Friends? Numerically small as we are, compared with the massed ranks of mainstream institutional religion, our beloved Society is uniquely placed to make a contribution. We have no creed. We never have, never do and never will insist that those who join us believe this or that - or if we do we betray our own tradition. We have no clerical hierarchies to enforce unanimity or conformity. We are not in bondage to the authority of scripture or a spiritual elite. We are seekers, cautious of those who loudly proclaim themselves finders. We claim to live adventurously and experimentally. Over the centuries we have rid ourselves of one dogma after another: Biblical inerrancy, atonement by blood sacrifice, the unique divinity of Jesus, his virgin birth and resurrection, Satan, Heaven, Hell, an after-life... All these are at best optional in modern liberal Quakerism. And so too is belief in other remnants of supernaturalism, not excluding a supernatural God.

In 1995 some three hundred Friends from Britain, Ireland, Europe and the USA met in Manchester to commemorate the centenary of the 1895 Manchester Conference, commonly regarded as a key moment in the transformation of the Society from nineteenth century conservatism to twentieth century liberalism. I was invited to give a lecture on the last night and I wondered what I could add to the several weighty speakers preceding me in reviewing the last hundred years of Quakerism. I decided to invite

Friends to imagine that we were meeting not in 1995 but 2095, looking back at the Quakerism not of the twentieth but the twenty-first century.

So I pictured a Society that, on the eve of the twenty-second century, had come to embrace "an expressionist, humanist or non-realist religious faith", confident in the understanding that "all religious faith - Catholic and Moony, Hindu and Native American, Rastafarian and Quaker, conservative and liberal - is created in human culture and by human imagination, matured in human history and celebrated in human language and human community"; that "religious values are wholly human"; and that "we must learn to get along without an absolute referent". I noted that although "the new understanding of religion as wholly human seems blindingly obvious from our late twenty-first-century perspective", it had been denounced a hundred years earlier as atheism and blasphemy, "or put down as sceptical reductionism or mere intellectual 'notions'". Nevertheless, the twenty-first century had seen Friends "joyfully relating their wholly subjective and metaphorical understanding of God not only to the faith of George Fox, James Nayler and Isaac Penington", but to the evolving circumstances of a changing world. I concluded:

Our own twenty-first century saw the deepening divide between pre-modern objective religion, where the natural and the supernatural diced with each other, and a post-modern subjective faith which carried forward the seventeenth-century Quaker project of wholly and radically incarnating God in the human spirit, dispersing the divine into humanity, extinguishing the old natural/supernatural dualism, and centring spirituality on human experience. From the 1990s, and on into the twenty-first century, Friends, along with the rest of the Christian tradition, and other faith traditions too, had to wrestle with the new light, which turned out to be only a fresh beam from the old Light of the World, powered by recharged batteries.

Yes, there was an element of tongue-in-cheek in this vision of a future nontheist Religious Society of Friends. The one thing we can be quite sure of is that the future will not turn out according to our rash, brash predictions. As we press on into the twenty-first century we shall meet challenges we haven't yet dreamt of, and find solutions to problems we could not possibly foresee. But if a warm, generous opening towards nontheist spirituality and a non-supernaturalist understanding of "the Spirit" is not part of our future development, I fear our Society will continue to live in its own comfortable but increasingly irrelevant past.

Boldly embracing nontheism would certainly change the Society. It would be foolish to pretend otherwise. And change can be uncomfortable, especially to those who love the Society as it is, with all its funny ways, and to those for whom religion is a search for comfort rather than a quest for truth. But change is nothing new to Friends. The Society is not what it was a hundred years ago, when it was not what it was a hundred years before that. We no longer walk the streets "naked for a sign", dress in the drabbest clothing we can find, address each other in archaic "thees" and "thous", or denounce music, drama and the arts as the Devil's inventions. We no longer disown those who "marry out", or those whose sexuality doesn't conform to the bigotries of the ancient authors of Leviticus and Deuteronomy. We no longer pretend to believe in George Fox's perfectionism, or his miracles, and we no longer feel compelled to defend his sometimes astonishingly violent invective against those whose experience gave them different convictions. We have moved on. Of course we have. The world has changed, and we too must go boldly where the adventure takes us: not into the world as it is, but into a place where we can more clearly see the world as it might be.

There is so much to do! So much in our divided, warring world, our atavistic religion, our polluted politics, our unexamined ways of thinking that we need to *subvert*! Where shall we find the society of rebels, agitators and outsiders, the partisan recruits to the underground army of subversion whose loyalty is pledged to the republic of heaven on earth? Who will choose to be Godless - for God's sake?

David Boulton *is a member of Brigflatts meeting, Kendal and Sedbergh MM, in Britain YM. A broadcaster, journalist and author, his books include 'The Trouble with God: Building the Republic of Heaven' (O Books, an imprint of John Hunt Publishing, Winchester and New York) and 'Real Like the Daisies or Real Like I Love You?: Essays in Radical Quakerism' (Dales Historical Monographs, Dent, UK). He is working on a study of current historical Jesus scholarship, 'Who on Earth was Jesus?', to be published in 2007. He has co-led workshops on Quaker non-theism/humanism at Woodbrooke, UK, and Pendle Hill, USA, and workshops on Quaker history and theology in the UK, USA, Australia and New Zealand. He edited 'Sea of Faith' magazine, 1992-2002, and is an Associate of the Westar Institute, Santa Rosa, California, and its 'Jesus Seminar'.*

What's a Nice Nontheist Like You Doing Here?

Robin Alpern

This is the question nontheists hear all the time. At least, the nice ones do! The question reveals fundamental misunderstandings. One is that religion equals belief in God. The word "religion" (from *re*, "again", and *ligare*, "bind") says nothing about God, but simply points to connection. Whether you bind to your self, your family, your community, a tree or bird, a God, or to Life, the Universe, and Everything, binding together is at the heart of religious or spiritual life.

Another misunderstanding is the notion that some individuals are religious or spiritual and others are not. The urge to connect is native to humans. No matter how that urge may be deflected or deformed, it remains at the heart of us.

Since the question continues to arise, and I *am* sometimes nice, here are my thoughts.

I hear several questions in the title. How in the world did a nontheistic person get involved in the *Religious* Society of Friends? What *is* a nontheist? What do you actually believe? How can you even *be* a Quaker without believing in God?

A spiritual journey

I have almost always been a Quaker, but I wasn't always nontheistic. My parents joined Rochester Monthly Meeting (New York Yearly Meeting) when I was about two, and enrolled me as an associate member. I was raised with traditional Christian beliefs about God. Being a literal child, I tried to imagine/feel a being which was infinite and existed forever. I would end up feeling dizzy! I also tried to figure out which parts of a person were "that of God".

These questions didn't perturb me. I loved being a Quaker, and I bragged at length to friends and strangers about the testimonies, history, activities and principles of Friends. There was no Meeting nearby, so my family worshiped in the homes of two other Quaker families, attended every Yearly Meeting, and occasionally went to weekend conferences. I remember mental games I played to keep myself from expiring of boredom during Meeting for Worship, which children attended for the full hour. I also remember fascination with religious figures and their lives.

As a three-year-old, I had a vision of Christ. When I suffered a bout of near-fatal scarlet fever, Jesus came to my bedside. He looked exactly like the man in the portrait at my friend's church. He kissed my cheek and told me I'd get well. When my mother later referred to this "dream", I hotly informed her it had really happened.

When I was about eight, I had a vision of the earth, shrunk to the size of a basketball, floating before me. From that vantage point, I saw clearly that all people share the same home and could get along together.

Somewhere in my teens, doubts about God crept in. I assured myself that millions of people over millennia of civilization can't have been wrong. (It turns out millions of people *can* be wrong: witness the mistaken belief that, because hunger and violence have plagued humans since our beginnings, they must be inevitable.)

There were ups and downs in my relationship with God in my twenties and early thirties. I remember a time when I was wretched about difficulties in my personal life, and desperate for some kind of help. It suddenly occurred to me this was precisely what people turned to God for. I am an outgoing person, who confides problems to family or friends. But I'm aware of the temptation to choose the confidante most likely to take my side, or suggest decisions I already want to make. I was excited to realize I could receive comfort and all-knowing wisdom from God.

A few years later, I woke one morning with an overwhelming delight at being alive. My first thought was that I was deeply grateful to God. When I attended Meeting for Worship that Sunday, the absence of any mention of God in the vocal ministry was troubling to me, and I shared a message encouraging Friends to speak up about God.

At the age of thirty, I married Bowen Alpern, a convinced atheist. Our wedding was under the care of Ithaca Monthly Meeting (NYYM). Bowen became an enthusiastic participant in the Society, and we sometimes argued about the nature and reality of divinity. I regarded him as simply unenlightened, or perhaps unaware of the deep spirituality that clearly motivated his life. Once I asked what he did in silent meeting for worship. (You see, I started out asking the question!). He said he contemplated each of the Friends present, and considered what, if anything, prevented full love between him and them. It sounded far more powerful than anything I, with my belief in God, ever attempted. But I was in no way swayed to his point of view.

Then in 1992 I read a tract written by a good friend, describing the offices of Christ. Jesus of Nazareth's functions as prophet, priest, bishop, shepherd, etc., had never been explained to me. In the midst of trying to make sense of them, I received an opening. Human beings need and want so much from life, we may be driven to invent a God or gods who can aid us. Possibly *everything* we believe about God derives directly from our own fears and desires.

This, of course, does not tell us whether or not God exists. But the opening revealed that most "religion" is about living inside a story made up for human convenience. Human beings make sense of life by forming concepts based on experiences. Then the concepts shape new experiences. My childhood idea of Jesus, including the image from my friend's church, informed my experience of a healing energy. Had I been brought up on the Indian story of Shakti, I probably would have seen her at my bedside instead.

I wanted to keep as far from story and as close to truth as possible. I didn't think I could necessarily know whether or not there is a God, and what is God's nature. In the absence of clear evidence, I decided the most honest way to proceed would be to live as if there is not a God, while remaining open to fresh truth.

What I mean by nontheism

That is how I came to be a nontheistic Friend. I use the word "nontheistic" primarily because "atheist" has such negative associations. "Atheist" actually means *without*, not necessarily *against*, God. Since I don't know if God exists, and since some good has been done as a result of belief in God, I am not opposed to God. But whereas some Friends might interpret feelings of rightness or wonder or love as caused by God, I would be likely to interpret them as arising from simple human mechanics and dynamics.

Another reason I often describe myself as nontheistic, rather than nontheist, is that it sounds less set in stone. It allows room for my changing ideas, and for dialogue with others of different views. Of course, I could use the term agnostic, meaning I simply don't know whether or not God exists. However, I feel I have gotten off a fence by deciding to live as if there is no God, so I want a label that reflects this.

Not infrequently I hear comments from theistic Friends suggesting I am suffering a "dark night of the soul". Others hint I have never known God, so I can't be expected to believe. I listen as openly as possible, not wanting to miss *anything*! Still, from my point of view, there's plenty of light and Life here! I quake in meeting, and elsewhere, from the overwhelming sense of being present, here and now. I feel more and more happy. The experiences of unity I had as a child blessed me with knowing experimentally that there is that which binds us all, eternally, in love. As an adult I'm learning everything I can about what nourishes human beings and fosters community, how obstacles arise and how to transform them into building blocks. I am often in tears at the beauty of the people and the world around me. I continue to have "unitive" experiences such as I did as a young person. At our Yearly Meeting sessions in 2000, when we celebrated Jubilee, I had a momentary vision of the perfection of our world. Intellectually I can't grasp this concept, but for those few seconds I knew it experimentally.

I thought I might need to give up my nontheist identity when I realized that I *do* believe in the overarching power of love. Many Friends declare God is love or goodness. Then why have different terms? Why not just say love, or goodness? The reason is there is a *story* whose name is God, and you are evoking the story, which goes beyond the meaning of love or goodness. I mistrust and even oppose so many elements of traditional stories of God that I still choose not to translate my life in terms of God.

I confess I was somewhat dismayed by our choice of title for this volume, because to me it implies the authors are merely tongue in cheek, while believing, deep down, in God. I have neither a deep-down belief nor a hope of one. While I respect belief in God, I went so far once as to suggest, semi-seriously, banning it from the Religious Society of Friends, on account of the poor behavior some devotees display (see "Why Not Join the Unitarians?", *Universalist Friends*, 1997, #28, 23-28 at www.nontheistfriends.org.). It doesn't seem to matter how much we know about devastating inhumanities performed in the name of God, believers still insist belief is a good thing.

This unassailability of the rightness and goodness of belief in God is another reason I reject belief. One Friend asserted she knows God exists, because she can feel it from the bottom of her toes. Suppose I say I know from the bottom of my toes that fairies exist? I would be laughed at, of course, but as soon as God enters the picture, you aren't allowed to question.

Nontheists tend to love to question, and acquaintance with a few hundred nontheistic Quakers over the past decade has shown me the huge variety of unbelief that is possible. No wonder we can't even agree on a title for our book! Indeed, it was the discovery of our vastly different atheist perspectives that led my father, Glenn Mallison, and my husband and I to try to test our views through a process of corporate discernment. This got us into a bit of trouble and a lot of fun and spiritual growth!

Sufferings

In 1994 our trio proposed a discussion on nontheism at New York Yearly Meeting annual sessions. After a number of conversations with the Coordinating Committee on Ministry and Counsel, the proposal was declined. We were told that the topic "strikes at the heart of Quakerism".

Persistent, if nothing else, we approached our Yearly Meeting conference and retreat center. The director readily agreed to host a conference the next year, recognizing that our theme was in keeping with "our diverse complexity of beliefs and practices". We excitedly arranged for co-sponsorship by the Quaker Universalist Fellowship (QUF), and leadership by Kingdon Swayne, past clerk of Philadelphia YM and published nontheist.

Later that year I announced to my Meeting that I did not hold a belief in God. This was the tiny Meeting to which we had moved after our marriage; the same Meeting where I had ministered that we should speak openly of the divine; the Meeting that had declined my husband's application for membership because of his avowed atheism. I was angry with the Meeting for rejecting Bowen's request, and for other unresolved arguments.

The Meeting was, predictably, discomfited by my anger and disclosure of unbelief. I had requested to transfer my membership to a more compatible Meeting, and four months went by without the transfer being approved. Then I was asked to meet with Ministry and Counsel. The committee presented a letter explaining that the Meeting was "very clear in its conviction that we cease to be the *Religious* Society of Friends without a belief in God". The letter affirmed that I was loved and cared for, and that it was with great regret and sorrow that "we are removing your name from our membership rolls".

Read out of Meeting? Over a decade later, my heart still pounds. The day after, I found myself scanning my skin for spots or some other anomaly. Because I surely couldn't be me if I were no longer a Quaker. For months I slept poorly, and sometimes couldn't concentrate by day. I flinched each time someone brought up the subject, for fear they would disown me too. I yearned for a Quaker cavalry, rushing in to say, "You can't remove Robin from the Religious Society of Friends!"

Meanwhile, QUF decided to withdraw its co-sponsorship of our conference, and the retreat center withdrew its sponsorship as well. Much later, we learned a weighty Friend had expressed outrage that the center had planned to host us. Unsure we could attract enough participants to cover the costs, we cancelled the workshop.

In 1996, Bowen, my dad and I offered a workshop called "Nontheism Among Friends" at the annual Gathering sponsored by Friends General Conference. The week-long program exceeded the maximum enrollment of thirty, and inspired several other meetings during the Gathering.

Not wanting to be branded the Quaker Nontheists (or Nuts), nor to limit the conversation to our style and perspective, we invited others to lead the workshop the following year. It has been offered every year but one since then, always drawing a full crowd, and I have had the pleasure of co-leading six more times. Over the past decade of workshops and other activities of the nontheist community, I've observed that a large segment of our Society is interested in questioning and exploring beliefs. Far from causing a rift, nontheist discussion has supported many, many Friends to participate more fully in their Meetings. The workshops have helped Friends recognize there is a spectrum of belief. They have supported me in many ways to see how the discipline of disownment furthered my spiritual journey.

The conviction that *all* differences between people can be resolved kept me trying for nine years to repair my relationship with the Meeting that removed me. While neither of us significantly changed our views, we did much to restore our friendship and respect for one another. I was supported to deepen the search by many, many individuals, as well as a faithful committee appointed by the Quarter when I appealed the disownment. The Meeting insisted I had not been disowned, simply removed from membership. I couldn't tell the difference. Despite pain and anger, I respected the Meeting for standing up for their truth. And I learned how things I had done had been hurtful. I still think the best outcome would have been for us to uncover our unity of purpose, principle, practice and love, while respecting differences in language and concept. That could have led to my membership being reinstated. In the end, though, I recognized the Meeting was not going to rescind its decision, and I needed to return to membership in the Society. Our family began attending another Meeting in the Quarter.

Atheology

Years ago, the belief there is "that of God in everyone" was the organizing principle around which all my Quaker understanding revolved. So I see why Friends wonder how you participate in meeting for worship or business meeting, or receive a leading or hold someone in the Light, without believing in God.

Here's a question I ask in reply. If a nontheist falls into the forest and nobody hears her speak, does anyone know she's a doubter? Can you tell someone doesn't believe in God just by watching? People sometimes claim belief in God is a required basis for morality, but it's perfectly obvious there are heinous criminals who are believers, who in fact commit atrocities *in the name of* God, while on the other hand there are nontheistic people who lead saintly lives. Early Friends had the wisdom, much of the time, to concern themselves with orthopraxy, right practice, rather than with orthodoxy, right belief. From my point of view, if a group of people are agreed on building a perfect city, it doesn't matter how they explain their inspiration and vision. They can agree on building materials, the layout, a timeline, and other details, and along the way, they can have wonderful conversation about different interpretations of who or what is guiding them, how and why they are guided, and all the other delightful thoughts we have about what on earth is going on here, anyway. In other words, we can build the city together whether we think we were called to do so by God, or whether we imagine we came up with the idea out of our own heads.

Some say they cannot in good faith worship with nontheistic Friends, because the latter are not "gathering" with the rest. As I've said, humans innately seek to join together. The nontheistic Friend may not formulate thoughts in meeting along the lines, "I adore God, I seek to know God's will, I thank God for all the blessings she has bestowed on me." Instead, this Friend may be contemplating the gifts and challenges of certain human relationships, or the beauty of nature, or principles of peace. The fact that the images, concepts and vocabulary of this Friend do not specifically refer to a traditional God should not stand in the way of the neighboring theistic worshiper, any more than should the grocery lists, sexual fantasies, to-do lists and general woolgathering occupying the minds of at least some of the other theistic worshippers!

If the difference between theist and nontheist lies only in how we interpret our religious lives, then maybe there is no point to writing further. However, I find great reward in thinking through and articulating how I perceive life works and what my part in it is. Conversation with others is a major aspect of my religious life. I offer here the fundamentals of my philosophy.

The basis of my understanding is that there is one life, one source, one being, one energy, which manifests physically as the universe we identify as planets, people, animals, rocks, water, air, etc.. This means I hurt when you hurt; I am uplifted when you are. It means I can hold someone in the Light, by focusing my attention on our innate connection, at a time when they may be feeling separate.

I care very much that this one stuff that makes up the universe *not* be identified as God. The notion of God is so old and freighted, so storified, that it stands in the way of my being present "in the life", as early Quakers said.

I view meeting for worship as a precious opportunity to become very present to the oneness of all humans, of all existence. I come there to rest in the peace available when I share space and time with people who are not busy talking and doing, and who are collectively, consciously, aiming to lift our hearts and minds as high as they'll go. I bring my concerns, knowing that sometimes, in the warmth and safety of meeting, something intractible will melt. There is a quality of our quiet togetherness that I recognize instantly, whether I am at home, or visiting for the first time in a Meeting across the country. In Paris Monthly Meeting, where I spoke the language imperfectly, I still *knew* that human huddle.

At times, I attempt just to feel the sense of the meeting. What is the exact nature or spirit, right now, of our Meeting?

A second principle of life, as I have experienced it, is that there is a direction at work. Again (are you surprised?) I resist naming this direction the will or purpose of God. I don't know for certain it isn't, but I don't think of it that way. For one thing, it's too easy to confuse the will of God with what I want or need. I'm not sure the universe cares. It seems more likely the universe is neutral, simply doing what it's doing. When we are smart, we figure out what the universe is doing (such as noticing that gravity isn't just a good idea, it's the law!). When we go along with the universe, things go better for us.

I balk when people say, about some tragedy, that we just don't understand the purposes of God. This can shield us from appropriately feeling our devastation, and hinder us striving to overcome disaster. Once a neighbor told me, after a pet died, that it was God's will. I felt the pull to be comforted. Another part of me, though, objected to being robbed of the chance to grieve fully, and also to consider carefully whether I might have handled the pet's care differently.

Still, it is apparent there is a movement or direction in life, whether on the small scale of shaping this essay, or on grander scales like development of a culture. What is the source of this force or movement? I don't know! Of course I wonder and theorize about it, but I return to not knowing. This does not persuade me to adopt a belief in God in order to answer my question. I don't know why my ball point pen works either; I just keep using it.

Ironically, one of my most powerful experiences of underlying direction was while facilitating a discussion of nontheism, with about thirty Quakers. Normally, I rely heavily on agendas and lists to stay on track. However, I hadn't had a chance to prepare queries or an outline. Nervous, I listened more intently than ever to the intial round of introductions. When we finished, a question rose in my mind. We considered it at some length, and then a new question came to me. Conversation went on in this way for the whole two hours. I felt as if I'd stepped into a river for a swim, and discovered that the current was so gentle, yet strong, that I could give up all my plans and just float along. I saw this as a manifestation of the natural forward motion of living beings, which we experience when we feel safe enough to open up.

A third principle of life is that there is often order built into the movement. Just as every normal human fetus develops through the same steps, the decision to paint the Meetinghouse purple arrives through an ordered progression. The purpose of meeting for worship with a concern for business is to do our best to perform the necessary dance. The sense of the meeting arises when everyone has joined in a vision. Not everyone necessarily describes the vision the same way, or shares exactly the same motives or emotions, and there can even be some who have a very different view. They may agree to hold it in dynamic tension with the common vision, by standing aside.

I recognize leadings and callings as the promptings that naturally arise when we do our various dances in life. It seems (look out, this will not be *nice!*) arrogant and perhaps even ignorant, to say "a *true* leading from God". Of course this goes back to our Quaker cultural view that there is "that of God" within us, and then there is *other* stuff. I have been strongly influenced by Siddha Yoga, an ancient Indian philosophy, which declares that "God dwells within you, as you". This exuberant perception seems to make our Quaker measure of godliness quite miserly. I regard all desires and fears as proceeding from the only source there is, and therefore all true. The trick is to figure out which promptings will best move the dance along.

A fourth principle is what has been popularly phrased "be here now". So simple, yet so difficult. Perhaps the greatest power I possess is to be who and where I am.

Epilogue

I arrived one First Day at the Meeting our family had been attending, and where many Friends had been encouraging me to join. Before entering, I was stopped by the clerk of our Care and Counsel Committee. "Please," she said, "just sign this." She handed me a sheet of paper on which was written, "Dear Friends, I request membership in Scarsdale Friends Meeting".

Those who have been reading carefully may not be surprised to hear I paused. "This isn't right," I thought. "Such an important letter needs to be lovingly crafted and full of the passion and pain and fears and cares I have about joining a new Meeting." Another stiller, smaller voice said, "Robin, just sign the letter".

Quakers, as we know, take their time doing business. But at rise of worship an hour later, three Friends introduced themselves as members of my clearness committee! "Wow," I thought, "the cavalry at last!"

At meeting for worship with a concern for business in June 2003, Scarsdale Meeting accepted me into membership. I was very moved when the Meeting minuted that "Robin has always been clear [for membership]" and "her disownment... was an improper over-reaction... We are particularly pleased that Robin's sense of unity with the Religious Society of Friends was not broken by her difficult experience, even as she retains the lessons she learned from it". This was balm, not only for me.

Abbe Pire is quoted by Erich Fromm: "What matters today is not the difference between believers and nonbelievers, but that between those who care and those who do not care" (*You Shall Be As Gods* , Holt, Rinehart and Winston, 1966, p54). I am drawn to people who are passionate about their religious life, even when we disagree on particulars. For myself, I find it most empowering to assume responsibility for who I am and what I'm up to. I do my best to avoid developing beliefs that will freeze my awareness and experience into concrete judgments, which will then bar the way to new experience and awareness. I stand ready at every moment to throw out everything I "know" in favor of that which is real and present, sometimes known as the truth. I will eat these words with relish – also ketchup and mayo – if they come between me and life!

Robin Alpern *is a member of Scarsdale Monthly Meeting, Purchase Quarterly Meeting, New York Yearly Meeting. She declares her primary work to be "raising my four beloved children, whom my husband and I home educate in the School of Benign Neglect".*

GODLESS FOR GOD'S SAKE

30

Something to Declare

Philip Gross

Here they sit. Like the clean but dowdy room around them, the people have a resolute unconcern for appearances. It is all mildly eccentric and a little quaint. There seem to be rules but where is the rule-book? Even so, there is something here I'm drawn to. There's an attitude of listening, though to what, I'm not sure. Twenty years on, I'm still here, and it is not a case of *they* but *we*.

Excuse this flashback in the present tense. I am trying to see what kept me. It was certainly not theology. I had never sat easy with doctrine in the Church of England as a child, or in Trotskyist groups in my twenties, and it was a relief to hear the hotchpotch of tones and beliefs in Quaker ministry. Better still, to see people listening to and somehow *through* each other's language, whether Bible-Christian or New Age or humanist-political. That seemed a good way to be.

And yet, a creeping unease. Is it consideration for the beliefs of others that leads so many of us to safely unspecific terms like "the Spirit", or is it a lack of plain speaking? When, after fourteen years, I applied for membership I was waved through, like at Customs, as if I had Nothing To Declare. It is good to be accepted, of course, but surely I *did* have something to declare? I was (am) not a Christian. I did (do) not see any reason to believe in any God outside the laws of nature and the workings of the (endlessly complicated) human mind.

These days I find myself sitting in the centre of the meeting, an elder, one of the Friends newcomers think *must* know what is going on. I can't get away with *Don't Know* any more. If *I* don't, maybe *nothing* is going on. If I think *something* is, then I should try to say it. In an organisation founded on belief in God, that must mean I "do theology".

God has come a long way since the early days of the Old Testament. The Judaeo-Christian Bible reads like the story of Him growing up, or of the collective mind that envisaged him growing out of fear of a stern despot, through wary respect for a father who smacks hard but knows what is best for us, into the Jesus stories where God lays aside authority and suffers with us. I sense that the next chapter is where God dissolves Himself in His creation, in us, and gives us grown-up responsibility. If He is a good father, then He wants us to leave home.

So God as story, albeit a rattling good one? Theist Friends might say it doesn't matter whether we see God as supernatural being or metaphor, as long as we can still *sense, and say, God*. Does it not matter equally to Friends like me, who declare ourselves humanists, yet engage with religion? We should have our bags searched: we *have* something to declare.

What am I listening for in meeting, if not the voice of God? Do I think it is just us doing it, like when as a teenager I played at a seance with friends? (We knew it was *one* of us pushing the wineglass, though if you'd asked we would each have said, sincerely, *Not me.*) I remember that, wryly, when meeting gathers and *the spirit speaks.*

So... are we talking to ourselves? But *ourselves* contain multitudes. It is neither revolutionary nor mystical these days to say that our conscious minds, the small circles of lamplight we call self, are just part of the picture, amidst the unvoiced messages of our bodies, and millennia of felt and thought experience in the languages we speak, the images we think in. As a writer, I know the heart-stop of the moment when a character I've been inventing turns round and announces *No, I wouldn't do that; I'd do THIS.*

For artists, making isn't *making up*; in whatever terms you choose, it is *relationship*. If I say God is a metaphor, I don't mean a figure in an allegory, made to stand for the thing we know it stands for. I mean an image, found or "given", with a deep life of its own, with resonances as yet undisclosed, maybe inexhaustible. This is actually very everyday. All our grandmothers knew that sleeping on a problem often finds an answer. You don't have to believe in mystic forces to know you can surprise yourself in your dreams, or be a paid-up Jungian to say that there is far more than one ego's experience somewhere down there in us all.

It is very human, the urge to get out of our small selves - in high art, religion, love, sports or binge drinking. It is not that hard to get "inspired". Not only embarrassing poetry but real historical atrocities are perpetrated in that state. When Friends sit together in a circle, it creates a fertile space between us from which leadings might emerge. It also calls for *discernment*. Early Friends soon found leadings sometimes lead to very strange places; they can come from many places in our minds. Which ones are "of God", we have to choose.

(Bible Christians might remember that the Bible was *selected* by the early church in, at worst, power politics, at best, discernment.)

I trust my instinct, to a point. *True* moments, in meeting, or with people or places, or in Buddhist practice with no God involved - feel like perspective, depth and clarity. They do not tell me what to think, but *how* it is possible to think it: an attitude towards the world inside us and outside us. And that is what I must have recognised, twenty years back, in that dowdy room. A way of sitting-with. I trust my instinct better when I'm part of it, with Friends. That doesn't seem much to build a theology on, but it might be everything.

Philip Gross *is a member of Redland meeting, Britain YM, and is a writer and Professor of Creative Writing at Glamorgan University.*

It's All in the Numbers

Joan D Lukas

Numbers seem to be everywhere, both in our minds and in the external world, from our earliest days on. We use them to count, to measure, to order, to compare. I have enjoyed thinking about them and working with them for as long as I can remember, as a young child, as a student, and as an adult mathematician. For almost as long, I have been curious about the nature and reality of numbers and of the mathematical enterprise. When mathematicians are at work, are they working as discoverers or inventors? I want to investigate these issues here, along with their connection to questions of theology.

Several questions arise in connection with the reality of numbers. Do they exist out in the world, waiting to be discovered? If so, where are they and how did they come to be there? Or are they created in our minds and imposed on the world? If we create numbers, what is the largest one that anyone has written down or thought of so far? Do numbers larger than this number exist or will they come into being only when they are conceived by a human mind? I remember that as a young child I had a competition with a schoolmate as to who could think of the larger number. We quickly tired of this game when we realized that there was no way to end it. In a similar vein, a story is told about a child who claimed that twenty-three was the largest number. When she was asked, "Well, what about twenty-four?" she concluded that she had been off by one.

If numbers and other mathematical concepts are mental constructs, are we free to construct these concepts in any way we choose? What constraints are there on the relationships among them? Could we decide that $2 + 2 = 5$? Could the result of multiplying two negative numbers be either positive or negative according to our preference?

These questions about numbers need not be a pressing concern for the working mathematician or the bank teller or anyone else who uses them in daily life. We can count, measure, order and compare as much as we like without asking what and where numbers are. But still the questions lurk and have puzzled many people, including me, for a very long time. These questions or closely related ones became hot topics among mathematicians at the beginning of the twentieth century. This was a period of deep investigation into the foundations of mathematics occasioned by startling new developments and the appearance of paradoxes. Mathematicians divided into several camps with very different formulations of the nature of number and of mathematical truth.

One answer to the question of the reality of numbers, an answer sometimes labeled "Platonic" after the philosopher of ancient Greece, holds that numbers and other mathematical concepts such as circles, lines and triangles, are objectively real and have their existence in an ideal universe of which the world of sense data is just an approximation. According to Plato, a line or circle we draw is an imperfect attempt at reproducing the ideal line or circle, which, like numbers and mathematical truths, exist independently of human acts and thoughts. We humans may discover the laws of arithmetic or the Pythagorean theorem, but they were true before we discovered them and would still be true if they remained undiscovered forever.

When mathematicians are engaged in their work in the medium of numbers and mathematical concepts, this Platonic view feels right. It feels to us that we are exploring a universe and discovering truths about it. Numbers, circles, and mathematical relationships feel at least as real as sense data. But when we step back from direct mathematical work and investigate the Platonic realist view itself, it does feel problematic. Where is this ideal universe? What is its relationship to the world we perceive through our senses? We may then pull back from the Platonic view and assert that numbers exist only in a formal sense, as symbols to be manipulated according to rules, like pawns in a game of chess. The rules of this game are constrained only by the requirement that they not lead to contradictions. This idea of mathematics as a formal game offers a way out of the tangle of issues about the ideal universe but it doesn't resonate with the way doing mathematics feels.

A third view, known as intuitionism or constructivism, emerged at the beginning of the twentieth century in response to some difficulties and paradoxes that appeared in the mathematics being developed at that time. According to this view, mathematical objects do not exist unless and until they are constructed by a human mind. A statement cannot be said to be true or false until we know which of these is the case. So, for example, it would not be correct today to say that either it will rain tomorrow or it will not. The restrictions that the constructivist view wishes to impose on mathematical reasoning would cause major changes in the way mathematicians work and the results that they are able to prove. In fact, L E J Brouwer, one of the originators of constructivist mathematics, renounced some of the theorems for which he became famous as a mathematician because they did not fit the constructivist paradigm.

Few mathematicians accept the constructivist approach to their field. It is too restrictive and insists on a too radical rewriting of the criteria for mathematical truth for most working mathematicians. For many of them, their "official" view of mathematical truth is the formalist one, holding that mathematics is a symbol manipulation game. But in their hearts, they adhere to the Platonist view of reality. According to the mathematicians Philip J Davis and Reuben Hersh, "Platonism was and is believed by (nearly) all mathematicians. But, like an underground religion, it is observed in private and rarely mentioned in public" (*The Mathematical Experience,* Birkhauser Boston 1981, p339).

So here is the situation mathematicians find ourselves in. We work with numbers and other mathematical concepts on a daily basis. They seem as real as anything else. But when we try to say how they are real and where they exist, difficulties arise.

And so it is with religious experience. Similar questions arise as to the existence and nature of something "beyond" that many call God. Many have held that this is an independent reality, existing before and beyond the world that we perceive. For others, the word "God" can only refer to a free creation of the human mind. Still others hold that the idea of God is a tool, used by some as a guide for human thought and action toward perfection and by others for oppression; it does not correspond to anything actually existing in or beyond our world. Are we constrained to believe either that God exists objectively and exactly as described in the Bible or the Koran or else that the concept of God is completely meaningless unless and until we choose to invest it with meaning? Many nontheist Friends have spoken and written about translating talk of God into personal or naturalist terms. If one doesn't believe in God as an eternal objective reality, what does it mean to carry out such translations?

The ideas of mathematical reality and theism have been connected in several ways. Some of the earliest mathematicians and philosophers have maintained that the idea of number is the most fundamental in the universe and that it offers connection to divinity. Pythagoras was an early Greek mathematician, whose name we heard in high school in connection with the Pythagorean theorem about the relationship between the lengths of the sides and hypotenuse of a right-angled triangle. For Pythagoras and his followers, mathematics and religion were one and the same. Their sacred symbols were mathematical and their motto was "All is number". More recently, it has been asserted that "God is a mathematician", that mathematics holds a perfection that can only be attributed to the mind of God. The Platonic idea of a transcendent universe in which numbers exist applies as well to God. In each case we are left with the same questions about the relationship between this universe and our everyday world, between these concepts and our own minds. And if I decide to reject the Platonic transcendent ideal of number, must I also reject the very idea of number? If I reject the transcendent God, must I also reject all religious impulse and perceptions?

There is a famous quasi-mathematical argument for belief in God, formulated by the philosopher Pascal, who was also one of the founders of the mathematical study of probability. Pascal presents the question of belief in God as a wager. His argument begins by saying that God either exists or does not exist and that we can choose to bet either for or against existence. If God exists, we will reap eternal rewards if we bet in favor of existence, and eternal punishment if we bet against it. If God does not exist, then it matters little which way we bet, for no reward or punishment is forthcoming in either case. Pascal's conclusion is that the only rational choice is to believe in God.

There are, of course, problems with Pascal's argument. It assumes that the God in question must be exactly as described by the Catholic theologians of his day. Might it be instead that God does exist but metes out rewards and punishments according to some criterion other than orthodox belief or unbelief? Faith might then offer no advantage or perhaps, perversely, even a strong disadvantage. Nevertheless, his argument is mathematically interesting because it introduces the idea of utility or expected value. Since Pascal's time, this idea has become an important ingredient of the mathematical theory of probability.

Mathematics and religion have been interwoven in practical ways as well. Christian scholars have invested in mathematics for the development of liturgical calendars and the determination of the proper times to celebrate religious events such as Easter. Muslims have developed some advanced mathematics to determine the proper direction to face in prayer. Mathematical concepts of zero and infinity have had an earlier development and a more welcome reception in cultures in which these ideas resonate with religious imagery than in cultures whose religions find them repugnant.

My personal religious and mathematical experiences reflect this historical and cultural interweaving. There is a relationship between my responses to the questions of the reality of religious and mathematical objects. Although I do not share the Platonic vision of an ideal universe as a home for mathematical objects, doing mathematics does not feel to me or, I suspect, to others who devote large parts of their professional and intellectual energy to it, like an arbitrary exercise or formal game. And, although I am not at all comfortable with the idea of a transcendent God somewhere in a part of the universe beyond our knowledge, I do feel that there is something real and meaningful to me in experiences that I believe others describe in theistic terms.

So where do I land as a non-Platonist mathematician and a nontheist Quaker?

The questions that have troubled me and other mathematicians and philosophers of mathematics are about the relationship between human minds and mathematical concepts. Must the existence of numbers be either totally independent of human thought or totally dependent on it? Or might the relationship be more complex? I face a similar dilemma with respect to the theist/nontheist question; am I constrained either to accept the idea of God as an eternal transcendent reality or to reject it along with all religious experience I seem to have? Or might there be another alternative? In both cases, total acceptance and total denial feel equally wrong. I believe that there is another way to look at these questions and that light is shed on them by current work in cognitive science and neuroscience.

As David Boulton has eloquently pointed out in *Real Like the Daisies or Real Like I Love You: Essays in Radical Quakerism"* (Quaker Universalist Group / Dales Historical Monographs, 2002), there are many ways of being real and concrete physical reality is not necessarily the most compelling of these. There is also much evidence from recent neuroscience research that the human brain contains specialized circuits or modules for particular kinds of intuition or knowledge. Some of these are specialized for mathematics. In his book *The Number Sense: How the Mind Creates Mathematics* (Oxford University Press, 1997) cognitive neuroscientist Stanislas Dehaene presents detailed evidence of independent modules related to mathematical understanding. One module, shared with other animals, is the basis for an approximate number sense that allows us to roughly distinguish among quantities. Another is a language-dependent module that is used in computation. Dehaene presents cases of patients with brain lesions that preserve one of these abilities while totally destroying the other.

There is also evidence from neuroscience research that there are parts of the human brain that are specifically activated during meditation, prayer, or other experiences perceived as religious. Research on these brain/religion connections are reported on by Eugene d'Aquili and Andrew Newberg in *The Mystical Mind: Probing the Biology of Religious Experience"* (Augsberg Fortress, 1999) and *Why God Won't Go Away: Brain Science and the Biology of Belief* (Ballantine Books, 2001). They discuss a section of the brain called the "orientation association area" that is responsible for orienting an individual in space and providing a delineation between the self and the physical space outside it. Their research provides evidence that the activation level of this area is decreased during deep meditation and prayer (*Why God Won't Go Away*, p7).

The evidence about the structure of the brain provided by neuroscientists provides a way to look at the mind and its relationship to concepts, including mathematical and religious concepts, that is more complex than either a blank slate on which experience is written or a willful constructor of experience. Neuroscience research shows that the brain is a complex structure of interacting abilities with specialized modules for different kinds of knowledge and abilities. Within cognitive neuroscience, researchers are focusing on some of these specialized areas. Among these is the emerging field of cognitive science of mathematics, treated in works such as *The Number Sense* mentioned above and *Where Mathematics Comes From: How the Embodied Mind Brings Mathematics into Being* (Basic Books, 2000) by linguist George Lakoff and psychologist Rafael E Nunez. There is much work yet to be done in this field, but scientists are concluding that certain mathematical concepts are built into our brains. Other neuroscience research, as described above, suggests a biological basis for religious experience.

These suggestions open the possibility, both for mathematical concepts and for religious ideas, of an alternative to the poles of transcendent reality, independent of human thought, and arbitrary invention by humans. Perhaps there is something real about these concepts but their reality is related to the way our brains, and therefore, our minds, work.

Joan D Lukas *has been a member of Friends Meeting at Cambridge, New England Yearly Meeting, USA, since 1989 and a professor of Mathematics at the University of Massachusetts Boston since 1967 (Professor Emerita since 2004). She has served on several Meeting committees and is currently a member of Ministry and Counsel and of Friends for Racial Justice. She attended the Nontheism Among Friends Workshop at the annual Gathering of Friends General Conference in 2000 and served as co-facilitator of the Workshop in 2001 and 2004. She teaches courses in mathematical logic, history of mathematics, and mathematics for teachers.*

Chanticleer's Call:
Religion as a Naturalist Views It

Os Cresson

We move. Sometimes we are moved and sometimes it results from our earlier movements. Some movements are private, only noticeable to the person moving. Some barely feel like motion. Talking and remembering are motions, as are sensing and experiencing.

Motions are physical events caused by other physical events. We are part of the ebb and flow of the universe. All is in motion, nothing stands still. Suns rise, birds sing, and poets write. The universe rolls along.

This is enough for naturalists who assume nothing exists but events we observe or reasonably infer from observations. Supernaturalists deal with other realms not observed or reasonably inferred. This requires its own languages, methods and tests of truth. For the naturalist, knowledge (that is, useful behavior) derives from observations of motions of the universe. From this we learn how to move more effectively through our lives. Gradually we change in the ways we move and we need support to continue to change.

As to what cannot be observed, naturalists respond by looking at its visible aspects. They assume the unseen works in much the same way as the seen until there is reason to assume otherwise. Tools may extend our range but eventually we come to a limit of knowledge. There the naturalist waits. While waiting we look around but we avoid speculating. Better to wait in silence.

Consider, for example, spiritual phenomena. These are always accompanied by physical events – that is how we know about them. Experiencing and thinking and talking about them are physical events. These are enough for the naturalist. The same is true of emotional reactions. Love for one another is as physical as a daisy.

Naturalists cannot be sure all this is true but it seems reasonable and no evidence contradicts it. They *are* sure good lives can be lived by people who view the world as physical cause and effect and nothing else.

The naturalists' approach is based on the way the world works. They seek to make statements that are useful. True statements are ones that work well. The meaning of a word is in the situations in which it is uttered. The meaning of a life is in its living. Values are what we have learned to work for. We seek ways to live well.

There are many sorts of naturalists. They vary in how far they extend the determinist principle – is anything undetermined, requiring a different approach? They also differ in language, keeping and translating some terms and avoiding others. Some naturalists share their views readily and others remain quiet because other efforts are more important to them. Naturalists are a diverse lot but there is a simple core to their approach.

For the naturalist, we are a causally determined physical system like a river, but this is a river that can enjoy itself, and observe and comment on itself, and foresee its future course, and modify that course. Observing this determined system is our starting point and everything else flows from it.

★★★

Nonphysical phenomena are popular today and have always been popular. Many people describe the experience of these phenomena, or have faith in them, or need them. They reject the naturalists' explanations, saying they are simplistic, or unsatisfying, or inadequate for a good life. This is not true. Staying grounded in the world presented by sense and reason can lead us to lives that are healthy, happy, wise, useful and caring. Naturalists assert they can live good lives and they acknowledge those who accept the supernatural can do so as well.

Religion is a combination of ethical standards and common purposes. It helps us hold to the standards and accomplish the purposes, and it offers rituals, including ritual explanations. The standards and purposes are not discovered in nature but are tested there. The rituals do not derive from the standards they accompany. Religious naturalists can, in all sincerity, behave as do their co-religionists. Harmony does not require agreement.

There is no topic that we must talk about with metaphors or supernatural concepts. Take worship: for some people this is about a relationship with the divine. However, nontheists worship in much the same way theists do. This is true of all areas in which the divine is said to play a role, as when we seek a sense of the meeting or discern our path or follow leadings. Theism is a fine way to view these activities but it is not the only way.

In any case, religious beliefs, faiths, creeds, and experiences are not as important as most people think. Knowing about the beliefs of others doesn't help us predict the rest of their behavior. Rather than being derived from one's religious faith, behavior is often learned directly. People can react appropriately to passing circumstances, whatever their history of religious experiences. Living well is a sufficient goal. This is religion centered on daily life instead of other realms.

Quakers are familiar with this focus on living. Those for whom God is central find God in their neighbors, making relations with them sacred. Some Quakers have pointed out that behaving like Jesus is more important than how we talk about him. We try to let our lives speak.

As chanticleer the rooster greets the sun announcing a new day, I call out to Quakers: your behavior is available to naturalist and supernaturalist alike!

★★★

In religion, psychology, education, law and science, theories are used to explain observations but the theories are on another level, never observed, spoken of in different terms, separate from the physical world they are said to explain. These otherworldly theories are rampant in all fields of human endeavor, partly because they are effective in many situations. Using faith as evidence is less work than observation, experiment and analysis and it is harder to argue against. Unfortunately, basing decisions on intuition can lead to trouble. Humans have evolved to quickly see how events are related, and we are quick to convince ourselves of relationships that do not exist. Concepts are created to explain observations that are the only evidence of the concepts. Reasoning is shaped by needs and emotions and the aversion to admitting ignorance or error. The entire human intellectual enterprise needs reform.

The naturalist proceeds in religion without God, immortality and spirituality. In psychology and education there is no need for mind, will, self and consciousness. In law, people are responsible for the consequences of their actions without ascribing those actions to free will.

In the naturalist's alternative, explanatory fiction is replaced by experimental study. This has been gradually accepted in astronomy, physics, chemistry and biology. Now it is the turn of human behavior, including the behavior of religious people. Naturalists see behavior controlled by surrounding environments rather than influences from other realms. Behavior is environment dancing with itself. This includes environments that are present and, in a sense, those of the future (that are expected, based on what has happened in the past). The past is included because we were changed by environments during our lifetimes and because environments selected the organisms that are behaving. In the environment is the origin of our species and the origin of our behavior.

For the religious naturalist, environment replaces God, self and mind. The environment requires us to act; it gives our lives meaning; it is comforter and arbiter; beginning and end; majesty and mystery; all credit belongs to the environments that shape our behavior.

Questions about the adequacy of this approach are answered by looking at the naturalist's life. Can a naturalist love a theist and vice versa? Let's try and see! Is there joy in worship shared by people holding different beliefs but united in love? Try and see!

★★★

We all know people whose religious views differ but who cooperate with each other and love each other. We have seen it happen. The future of humankind requires that we get better at it. Naturalists do this by focusing on how the world works. Common ground is found in the particulars of our lives. We all breathe and cry and smile. These are physical reactions to surrounding circumstances. We share the physical world; here we can find purposes to unite our communities.

Living with diversity can be a challenge. One key is genuine, outgoing toleration. We can look for what each other has to offer and support each other in our searches. We can accept concepts in our listening and reading vocabularies even when they are not in our speaking and writing vocabularies. We can accept that people speak differently, and respond to the source of their words, to the function rather than the form. We can let speakers speak and listeners translate, and let the test of speaking and translating be the communities we build.

A membership decision in a doctrinally diverse religious community, such as a Quaker meeting, can be a cooperative effort to discern whether applicant and community are working well together, whether they are in unity. One way to establish unity is to insist everyone accept one set of beliefs, but there are other ways. Unity can derive from common purposes, or it can be directly taught. The commitment to move forward together is worth much more than agreement on points of doctrine. We can find strength in diversity instead of creating problems by suppressing it. Unity is not a precondition for love - it arises as love goes to work.

In all these efforts, naturalists have an advantage because they are centered on the particulars. They define spiritual matters in practical terms rather than trying to link spiritual and physical phenomena. They naturalize religion rather than spiritualizing nature. The particulars of our lives and the purposes we work toward can unite a community. The naturalists' faith is ready for practical application. There is hope that a good life can be achieved. The naturalists' approach provides a basis for cooperation within a faith community and with people of other faiths.

★★★

Pleasantly, naturalists are found in many religions. I grew up as a Quaker, but I could have been a nature loving Jew or Buddhist, Sufi or Pagan, Catholic or Moslem... I treasure the silence of Quaker worship, the spontaneity of messages building one on another, the way all present share in leading the worship. I love Quaker honesty and simplicity and the response of Quakers to violence and injustice. Kindliness is offered to all.

These behaviors, so important to me as a Quaker, are also present in other religions. We all meditate, one way or another. We all come back to the ideals of the Golden Rule and the Sermon on the Mount. It is true that relations vary between naturalists and their co-religionists. Some naturalists are openly welcomed; some are welcome if they avoid mentioning their views; some need to separate themselves from the main body of their faith. Let us dedicate ourselves to loving and supporting each other, views and all, and to pursuing our common purposes.

Religious naturalists don't need to convince others to change their views. We do need to show that naturalists can live religious lives and that we merit inclusion in religious gatherings.

It is time for meetings, churches, synagogues and mosques to extend the blessing of membership to those for whom the physical world known through sense and reason is sufficient. The belief that the universe is a reliably functioning physical system, and nothing else, need not be reason for exclusion.

Let those who are clear on this say to the world that naturalists are welcome in their hearts and in their communities. This will encourage others to raise the concern. Religious people need no doctrinal barriers. We only need love.

Os Cresson *is a member of Mount Holly Monthly Meeting of Philadelphia Yearly Meeting in the USA, where he is Recording Clerk and a member of the Worship and Ministry Committee. In the past he was Recording Clerk of Burlington Quarterly Meeting and served on the Environmental Working Group and the Library Services Group of the Yearly Meeting. He served as co-leader of the 'Nontheism Among Friends' workshop at the Friends General Conference Gathering in 2001 and 2004.*

Further Reading:

The title came from two sources: the epigraph of Henry David Thoreau's 'Walden; or, Life in the Woods': "I do not propose to write an ode to dejection, but to brag as lustily as chanticleer in the morning, standing on his roost, if only to wake my neighbors up" (Boston: Ticknor and Fields, 1854), and the title of a paper that opened the way for a naturalist's approach to psychology similar to the one I propose for religion: 'Psychology as the Behaviorist Views It' (John B. Watson, Psychology Review, 1913, 20, 158-177). For more details please go to www.nontheistfriends.org and look for the annotated version of the essay, above, and another titled 'Quaker in a Material World' (published in Quaker Theology, 2003, 5(1), 23-54). Also see 'Quakers, from the Viewpoint of a Naturalist' (Friends Journal, March 2006).

Mystery: It's What we Don't Know

James T Dooley Riemermann

There is enough mystery in an acre of land - indeed, in the patch of soil beneath your feet as you stand in your garden - to hold the human race in awe until the day of our extinction. The more we learn about the complex and subtle dynamics of life, matter and energy that dance everywhere we look, the clearer it becomes that the old scientific dream of complete understanding is just that - a dream. The way of science has made discoveries of immense importance, and will presumably continue to make them, but at every turn the path of scientific discovery shows us even greater mysteries - which is to say, more things we are aware of but don't understand.

The past century of discoveries in atomic and subatomic physics reveals that the most physically dense objects in our everyday world are made almost entirely of empty space, in which infinitesimal particles whirl around one another at unimaginable speeds. At the smallest scale, we cannot tell whether some of these are particles or non-particle waves, or both simultaneously, or either depending on our method of observation. Our attempts to measure the movement of some of these particles seem to suggest that they exist in many locations simultaneously, further challenging our notions of what speed, space and matter are, along with Einstein's hallowed and well-tested rule that nothing can exceed the speed of light. None of the rules that hold in our everyday world seem to hold here. The qualities we perceive in the everyday objects before us relate as much to patterns of energy, and complex relationships between infinitesimal particles, as to distinct qualities of the objects themselves.

Following Einstein, our intuitive sense that physical objects move through essentially passive and substanceless fields of space and time is shattered. Rather, objects warp the space and time they move through, and objects of sufficient mass and density - theoretically, and perhaps in reality - can stop time completely. It is widely held that our universe began when an infinitely small point of frozen time exploded, and started the clock of our physical reality. The same theories project that our universe may end in another point of frozen time.

Of all the mysteries which resist our intelligence, perhaps the greatest is the one that gave rise to intelligence and mystery itself - consciousness. Or, more precisely, self-awareness - the usually unshakeable sense we have of ourselves as distinct beings.

Human beings know the experience of having or being a "self" more intimately than we know anything else; everything else we say we know is an assumption based on the subjective experience of that self. We have methods for distinguishing between those experiences that reflect the external world, and those that reflect the inner world of the mind, but those methods are imperfect, and in some forms of mental illness they disintegrate. In fact, as noted earlier, the physical world is not really the way we perceive it except in a vague, analogical sense. Color is not what we perceive it to be, nor the solidity of objects, nor the intuitive distinction we make between time and space.

Neurological studies demonstrate beyond any doubt the essential connection between the biological and chemical processes of the brain, and consciousness. It is no great trick to elicit certain types of mental experiences by stimulating certain parts of the brain, and moods can be changed in radical ways by introducing chemicals into the body which affect receptor sites within the brain. Studies of brain-damaged patients show how physical alteration of the brain can radically alter everything a person considers to be their "self". In more extreme cases of brain damage the self all but disappears. There is no objectively certain way to confirm this, but everything we have learned suggests that, with the total cessation of any chemical activity in the brain, the self ceases to be.

At the same time, it would be a gross overstatement to say we know what the self is, or the mind, or self-awareness. We can associate such mental phenomena with biological events in a fairly crude manner, but we don't *really* have the foggiest idea why we experience these phenomena, or if we could function without them, or at what point in our evolution from single-celled organisms to modern human beings we first reflected on our own existence. At which point everything changed.

Yet, for most of the human race, this unfathomable mystery of the natural world has apparently not been mystery enough. Throughout the centuries we have felt compelled to assert the existence of an unknown realm of mystery beyond that of the realm we can hold in our hands, see with our eyes, taste with our tongues, reflect upon with our minds. There must be something more, we insist. A transcendent mind, a power behind everything. For want of a better term, God.

★★★

Virtually every mature religious tradition has had its popular versions, drenched in magical thinking and superstition, and these versions have been the essence of religious life for most people at most points in known history. In the Christian tradition, the popular versions have tended to envision God as a human-like being of unlimited power, goodness and knowledge, who knows and loves each of us personally, and guides the world perfectly (with some wiggle room for human free will, which comes in handy to explain the existence of suffering in a world ruled by such a good god.)

Most, if not all, religions have also had their mystical traditions which, while not necessarily rejecting theological specifics and supernatural beliefs, tend to spend more time focusing on practices intended to evoke direct experience of the divine or transcendent realm. Even if this mystical tradition is the far lesser tradition in terms of numbers, one could make a strong case that the greatest spiritual leaders and writers in religious history have followed the mystical thread of their religion. One could also make a strong case that the greatest scriptural works were created as poetry, dealing with the experience of being human in the world, and only later were taken to be historical accounts of an actual God.

Today's best-known progressive Christian writers, along with many Quakers, follow this mystical thread. One might oversimplify such beliefs as "soft theism," where most of the specific claims of traditional or orthodox Judeo-Christian theism are dismissed, or at best ignored - angels, heaven, hell, a human-like being who created and guides the world we live in and loves each of us in a personal manner, prayer as a method for bringing about desired events and keeping disaster from the door. At the same time, soft theism tends to retain faith in the broadest and most comforting aspects of the old belief systems: the universe exists for a beneficent purpose, and our existence has an ultimate meaning that will not end with our death, nor even with the end of the human race.

The point of this criticism is not to prove such claims to be false. They cannot be proven false, and in fact the less specific the language used to express the claims, the less meaning words such as "true" or "false" have. If one experiences life in the world to be meaningful, that is one's experience. One could then question whether that experience reflects the nature of the world outside of human experience, but what of it? We are human, are we not?

Rather, the point is to explore the possible motivations for such beliefs. Have we reached toward truth (meaning, that which is the case) with all our strength, or is the well-documented human desire for comfort and security distracting us in our search for truth?

One motivation might be that the notion of a purposeful creator might serve to explain how such a fantastically complex and interrelated universe could have come to be. Rather than resign ourselves to partial, finally unsatisfying answers about the birth and nature of the universe, we can comfort ourselves that, whatever the details of creation, it unfolded because of the creative will of God. What had brought forth a frustrating sense of bafflement, is seen through faith as the perfect plan of a perfect will.

The trouble is, while such a faith might ease our discomfort and confusion, nothing has been explained at all. Everything we didn't know before, we still don't know. By saying God created it all, we have answered no questions, but merely added another huge, unexplainable entity to the long list of things we can't explain: the creator.

★ ★ ★

The most progressive modern theology is boldly stretching the boundaries of that perspective. Bishop John Shelby Spong, while expressing faith in something he chooses to call God, expressly rejects the long-standing theistic image of God as a distinct entity with a personality, and even more vehemently rejects the notion of a God who rewards good and punishes bad behavior, and the image in Genesis of a humanoid super-being who magically creates a world and has conversations with its denizens.

In *Why Christianity Must Change or Die* Spong spells out in painful detail the historical battering of the theistic notion of God, first by Copernicus, then by Galileo, Newton, Darwin, Freud and Einstein. First to fall, Spong observes, is the notion of a realm in the sky in which God resides, ruling over Earth as the center and Crown of Creation. Further discoveries underscored how insignificant Earth and humanity is in the context of the physical universe, and how humanity itself - in all likelihood the only species on Earth to conceive of God - evolved over eons from microscopic organisms without minds or hearts. Then, the exploration of the human mind dismissed the notion that our morality was handed down by the creator and ruler of the universe. Spong writes,

The theistic definition of God as a personal being with expanded supernatural, human, and parental qualities, which has shaped every religious idea of the Western world, came into existence not through divine revelation, Freud argued, but out of human need. Today this theism is collapsing. The theistic God has no work to do. The power once assigned to this God is now explained in countless other ways. The theistic God is all but unemployed.

This is a bold theological move, firmly rejecting traditional notions of God, and, in contrast with other progressive theological writers such as Karen Armstrong and Marcus Borg, acknowledging that these magical, anthropomorphic notions are, in fact, traditional and ancient. A disconcerting tendency among Armstrong, Borg, and others, is to assert that literalistic notions of God are a relatively modern innovation brought forth by the scientific mindset, rather than the more obvious explanation that the scientific mindset is still in the slow process of destroying a literalistic mindset that had dominated religion for millennia. Armstrong writes in *A History of God* that "...once the scientific spirit had become normative for many people, it was difficult to read the Gospels in any other way. Western Christians were now committed to a literal understanding of their faith and had taken an irrevocable step back from myth: a story was either factually true or it was a delusion." Later, critiquing the theology of Milton's *Paradise Lost*, she writes that "God comes across as callous, self-righteous and entirely lacking in the compassion that his religion was supposed to inspire. Forcing God to speak like one of us in this way shows us the inadequacies of such an anthropomorphic and personalist conception of the divine. There are too many contradictions for such a God to be either coherent or worthy of veneration." It's a fair criticism, but one that can be even more easily levelled against the Bible.

Armstrong rightly calls attention to a long mystical religious tradition that warns against focusing on literalistic images of God, and which advocates an approach of myth, mystery, and direct religious experience that intentionally defies direct description. What she seems to overlook is, these mystical traditions were never representative of the mainstream of religious belief, but rather were critiques of a mainstream that was for the most part intensely idolatrous and literalistic. The fact that myth and mystery played a crucial role in the great monotheistic religions does not mean that their adherents did not believe in the literal existence of the largely anthropomorphic God of *Genesis* and *Exodus*, or the Biblical characters who had occasional conversations with the creator of the universe. If there's one thing we know about almost all ancient cultures, it is this: they liked their magic.

Similarly, Marcus Borg, in *Meeting Jesus Again for the First Time*, writes that

The modern worldview, derived from the Enlightenment, sees reality in material terms, as constituted by the world of matter and energy within the space-time continuum. The experience of spirit persons [such as Jesus, in this example] suggests that there is more to reality than this - that there is, in addition to the tangible world of our ordinary experience, a nonmaterial level of reality, actual even though nonmaterial, and charged with energy and power. The modern worldview is one-dimensional; the worldview of spirit persons is multidimensional. Moreover, this other reality, it is important to emphasize, is not 'somewhere else.' Rather, it is all around us, and we are in it.

Like Armstrong, Borg implies that the rise of scientific understanding gave rise to literalistic religious understandings, rather than the far simpler explanation that the scientific understanding of the enlightenment was undermining an ancient, literalistic understanding of God as a being in the sky, an understanding which has been fighting desperately for its life ever since. Before that, the existence of a literal, personal God was rarely questioned, though often augmented with a more mystical understanding.

Spong, who readily admits that Western religions have always been magical, superstitious and literalistic in practice, nonetheless seems to fall a bit short of grasping the full implications of his rejection of theism and superstition. Again, *in Why Christianity Must Change or Die*, he writes:

If God is no longer to be conceived of as a 'personal other,' does that mean that the core and ground of all life is impersonal? Does this make God less than personal or mysteriously even more than personal yet still beyond our limited human categories and understandings? Such questions ultimately cannot be answered. They do, however, elicit a series of other questions. Does not the being of God manifest itself in intense personhood? Can one worship the Ground of Being in any other way than by daring to be all that one can be? Can one worship the source of Life in any other way than by daring to live fully? Can one worship the Source of Love in any other way than by daring to love wastefully and abundantly? Are there any categories that could be said to be more personal than those calling each of us into being, into living, and into loving? Would a life that reflected these qualities not be seen to reveal the image of God that is within that person?

These questions are purely rhetorical, in the sense that Spong implies his preference for answers that suggest a universal force of love. The first two questions are skeptical at a glance, and Spong dismisses them as "unanswerable," meaning we cannot answer "yes, God, the Ground of Being, is impersonal". The rest of the questions are hopeful, and it is clear that Spong desperately wants to answer "yes, God, the Ground of Being, is personal and loving". For the moment he stops short of giving that answer outright, but in the epilogue of the book he gets over his caution and states: "God, the source of love, calls us all to love wastefully." Good advice indeed, but in fact it is Bishop Spong, not the Ground of Being, who offers it. Spong rejects the traditional, theistic conceptions of God, but in the end nostalgia overcomes him, and he cannot bring himself to reject the unsupported but comforting notion that God, the Ground of Being, loves us.

★ ★ ★

A common theist critique of nontheism is that disbelief in "something more" reflects the arrogant assumption that what humans can see and measure is the be-all and end-all of reality. On the contrary, no reasonable nontheist - atheist, agnostic, humanist, naturalist - believes that human knowledge encompasses all of reality, or even comes close. It is the scientific worldview that utterly depends on a keen, rigorous and critical distinction between what we know, and what we do not know. What we can observe, examine, grasp, measure - that is what human beings can know. The rest we cannot know. A claim to knowledge of a realm beyond the one we live in, on the other hand, could be described as arrogance. If in fact there is some divine realm apart from the world we live in, all we can honestly say about that realm is that we do not know it, because we do not live in it. We live in the physical world. A world which, once again, contains enough mystery to keep us in awe forever.

Before Galileo could overturn the Genesis-inspired conception of Earth as the center of the universe, he had to humbly admit that he did not know where the earth was, regardless of what he had been led to believe for all his life. Then he observed the sky with great care, and shared the story it told him.

A distinction must be made, too, between "*something* beyond our knowledge" and "*things* beyond our knowledge". The former doesn't merely acknowledge that there is a great deal that we do not understand - an obvious truth. It implies that, at some level, the highest or most fundamental level, there are not diverse and interrelated truths, but One Transcendent Truth. This claim is made despite the fact that everything we have learned about the world reflects not unity but diversity and relationship - distinct, powerful and subtle forces that wrestle, dance and collide with one another. In all but a few tiny corners of the universe, this violent crashing has come to nothing we would value. In rare places such as our earth, the crashing results in a breathtaking dynamic equilibrium in the exchange of energy, where success builds on previous success, and the web of life struggles against the entropy that will eventually destroy it. Almost everywhere else, entropy has already won.

So, of course there are things beyond our knowledge, many of which will remain so forever: the origins of the Big Bang; the function and origin of many subatomic particles; exactly how it happens that we experience thought, sensation, emotion; the scientifically unsupportable but crucially human sense that one is a person with a soul.

One might ask, what does all this mystery mean? Many who profess some sort of faith in God insist it *must* mean something, that beyond the veil of everything that baffles us there must be "something more," something unified, coherent, and above all, meaningful. The mysteries themselves are trotted out as evidence for the existence of this unspecified "something more". (As Hamlet said, "There are more things in heaven and earth, Horatio, Than are dreamt of in your philosophy". By which he meant that Horatio should believe in ghosts.)

But why? Why would that which is beyond the veil of mystery be any more "divine" or "ultimate" or "spiritual" than that which we already know? The veil of mystery is simply the limits of our knowledge. There is the stuff we know about, and the stuff we don't know about. There is no particular reason to believe that the stuff we don't know about is any more divine than, say, a rock, or a chicken, or a Ford Fiesta. So the distinction between that which we understand or have direct experience of, and that which is forever beyond our knowledge, is by no means the distinction between the sacred and the profane, the spiritual and the material. It certainly provides no evidence of a transcendent realm. It is good and interesting and sometimes even fruitful to humbly reflect on the depth and breadth of our ignorance, but to take what we don't know and mystify it as divine is not likely to be fruitful.

So, then, is it meaningless to speak of the sacred, the spiritual, the holy, in our lives? Or is there a genuine and naturalistic way of speaking about the most rare and beautiful aspects of our lives without implying that we have thereby uncovered the ultimate meaning of the universe, or that the universe loves us? I think that there is.

★ ★ ★

Rarely do I feel led to use the word "God" to describe anything I experience, though I often relate deeply to what many fellow Quakers describe as God. Part of my reluctance stems from the fact that the word feels so terribly imprecise, and I can almost always find better ways to express myself. It's not a matter of simply replacing the word God with another phrase (the Divine, the Inward Light, the Christ Within, Love, the Ground of Being) but of taking all the language at my command and struggling to express how the world seems to me. Even then I come up short; the words rarely if ever capture the experience, but they come far closer than any timeworn, hand-me-down phrase that is likely to mean a thousand different things to a thousand different people.

When the most thoughtful believers speak to me of God, it almost always comes through to me as a heightened awareness of relationship. Grammatically, God is a being, an entity, but what Friends tend to describe as God seems more like an event, an encounter, that occurs when a self-aware individual becomes intensely aware of relationship - with another human being, with a community of Friends, with the complex web of beings and resources that sustain life on earth, with the sun that feeds energy to that web, with the entire cosmos out of which emerged absolutely everything we value. What a breathtaking moment is that encounter! Here I am, living my life as if I were a single soul, a person, a mind mysteriously sprung from a physical body. And in an instant it dawns on me that I am not just myself. On the contrary, the energy of the universe flows through me, and at my death will pass through me and back into everything that exists! My God! This is no metaphor, there is nothing magical or supernatural about it, nor is it something more out there with which I can occasionally commune. Rather, it is the essential, undeniable, literal, constant reality of being human in the real world. We are a part of everything, and it is all linked together.

For the moment, let's call it God. It may or may not be eternal, but it certainly began long before I was born, before life of any kind emerged, and it will live well beyond all of us. What, then, is the experience of God? As mentioned earlier, everything we have learned about the mind powerfully suggests that it is inextricably linked to the physical brain. When the brain is altered, happy people become sad, brilliant people become dull, gentle people become angry and violent, and sometimes entire personalities vanish without a trace. There is every reason to believe that our experience of God - that is, everything we can possibly know of God - will end with the death of our bodies. And when there are no more conscious creatures in the universe, there will be no experience of God. As far as anyone is concerned, no God. Ashes to ashes, dust to dust.

And there goes hope, there goes eternity, there goes nostalgia, there goes the happy ending we all yearn for. It will not do to pretend we are not disappointed. Part of that ineffable mystery of self-awareness is a built-in longing for eternity, for a connection with ultimate meaning. We don't know why we have it, but we have it. It will not do to deny that longing, nor to nostalgically pretend we have not learned what we have learned.

Yet, right now, for a while, we have ourselves, we have each other, and we have the world. The vast, quite possibly meaningless universe out of which we emerged, and into which we will dissolve, is in our hearts, our minds and our souls, alive with meaning.

James Riemermann first attended Twin Cities Friends Meeting, Northern Yearly Meeting, USA, in 1990. He became a member in 1995, and has served on Ministry and Counsel, Adult Education, News, and other standing as well as clearness and support committees.

Living the Questions

Sandy Parker

'All Truth is a shadow except the last, except the utmost; yet every Truth is true in its kind. It is substance in its own place, though it be but a shadow in another place (for it is but a reflection from an intenser substance); and the shadow is a true shadow, as the substance is a true substance.' - Isaac Penington, 1653. Britain YM Quaker Faith and Practice, 27.22).

The dominant emphasis of Quaker tradition is that it is "not a notion but a way" - and "this we know by experiment" (that is from our experience): so similar to the opening words of Dao, "the way that can be named is not the way". In this essay I consider how such paradoxical mysticism has informed and permeated my 70 years of life.

My story

I begin by presenting some of the warp and weft of the tapestry of my 70 years of "lived experience". I revisit my childhood and student days, my work as an educator, and my writing of the past 50 years. I gain a strong sense of coherence, continuity and congruence that goes back to my teens and to early childhood.

My Quaker grandmother's influence was strong, though never dominant. Her interest in the Theosophical Society ensured that it was a universalist influence, and her three children were sent to Quaker Schools. I followed in their footsteps. Yet my (Presbyterian Elder) grandfather's deep acceptance and affirmation of my being was at least as strong.

In my late fifties I discovered a letter he had written when I was but six years old - to a niece in Melbourne, Australia. War-time censorship restricted him to family news, and he tells of visiting my parents. I was sent to bed as punishment for some misdemeanour, and he offered to carry me upstairs. I kicked his shins, I beat a tattoo on his chest with my fists. The following day, both my parents being out to work, he was looking after me and asked what I might like to do. He wrote with obvious pleasure that I asked if we could fight like we had the night before! What comes over in his letter is strong delight in, affirmation of, my being, of my independence, of me.

At the age of seven I was sent to a small Quaker School at Yealand Conyers on the edge of the "1652 country" in north-west England, surrounded by Quaker history. The school was established in 1940 by Friends from Manchester and Oldham to provide a safer "Friendly" environment for the evacuation of their children from the war-zones that many British cities became. My dominant experience there was of belief in me, and in my potential as a human being in the way that my grandfather so lovingly showed. That wonderful small school closed in 1944 when no longer needed. I remember especially Elfrida Foulds' wide repertoire of Quaker stories, and her delight in Psalm 121:

I will lift up mine eyes unto the hills,
From whence cometh my help.

Misunderstanding the intention of the psalmist - that our salvation was not to be found in the hills but in God - I heard it as a question. For me, the mountains - whether of the Pennines (on a clear day we could see the distinctive silhouette of 2,700 ft Ingleborough from Yealand), or the nearby Lakeland Fells, or my native Scotland, became an ever present source of strength and help. And that set a pattern - there have always been places of particular power and energy for me - be they ancient stone circles, places hallowed by centuries of prayer and community like Iona, or the solitude of moors and desert.

I went on to attend two other Friends' schools, Ackworth and Bootham. I was not an easy pupil. When I was 17 a teacher enquired of me whether it might be possible for me "to observe some of the school rules some of the time"! Yet there was an underlying valuing of our individuality - even if it could, at times, be idiosyncratic or maverick.

I remember some who spoke to us at our Sunday "Evening Readings" - Jack Hoyland, of his work for peace in Spain and elsewhere; Reginald Reynolds, of his love of India and his meetings with Gandhi; crystallographer Kathleen Lonsdale briefly imprisoned for her opposition to war. Perhaps not their words, but certainly more than Jack Hoyland's booming voice filling the school Meeting House, and more than Kathleen Lonsdale's frizzy hair!

Tom Green, then Head of Bootham, seemed to rejoice that most of his senior students were agnostic - this in a man of deep personal Christian faith. He valued and encouraged strong independent thinking in his students, yet disciplined by an awareness of community - the essence and strength of Quaker tradition.

Formal teaching was largely conventional. I learned that "correct answers" earned marks, certificates, progress up the ladder of exam and career success: "questions" didn't (unless they were the "right" questions, and really answers disguised as questions). And I was mostly good at the answers! But there also shine a number of occasions when I was enabled to discover that questions were more important than answers, that with questions I could grow and explore, whereas answers could often be cul-de-sacs. I learned (mostly outside the classroom) that there were times, people, and places that were full of energy, of questions that tempted answers, which with patience and silence and space led on to other questions and to deeper knowledge and understanding. I discovered the communication of shared silence could hold more meaning than a thousand words, and that sometimes if I "answered" questions I could trap myself in the web of another person's answers and expectations.

Leaving school, I deliberately chose national service in the Royal Air Force rather than registering as a conscientious objector for alternative service. My life experience was enriched by encounter and friendship with people from backgrounds radically different from my own. I discovered the strength of small group companionship and exploration inherent in the Methodist tradition. I faced the full consequences of my decision to do military service when required to service aircraft with nuclear capability, finding support in my dilemma both from the Methodist chaplain, and from Quaker groups.

Beginning a university degree in chemistry, I became deeply involved with the ecumenical movement (through the Student Christian Movement), and found a spiritual home in the openness of the small groups of the University Methodist Society (there did not seem to be a place for me amongst Young Friends - perhaps on account of my conscientious military service).

Tiring of the physical sciences after years of specialisation at school, in the RAF, and at University, I sought an alternate course for my third year. Unexpectedly I found this in an intensive year of theology - with, as tutor, John Robinson, later to become known for his *Honest to God* and for giving evidence for the defence in the Lady Chatterley trial! Again unexpectedly, I found myself training to be a teacher of "religious education" (with chemistry as my second subject!). Now involved with the Methodist and Anglican traditions and the burgeoning ecumenical movement, I began to appreciate the strong underpinnings of Quaker vision in the experience of being part of the radical educational and spiritual community of Yealand Manor School as a seven and eight-year-old. The Jesuits may say "give me a child until (s)he is seven", but the two-year experience of that community has been a determinant of my life's direction and philosophy.

Leaving university, I began teaching in grammar and comprehensive schools. Almost by accident I moved to spend 18 years in a Quaker school, though my commitment had been to public-sector maintained schools. In the world of teaching in which I was now immersed, religious education went through a series of phases and fashions. "Religious Instruction" became "Religious Knowledge", as it was realised that "instruction" and nurture into a particular religious and cultural tradition were inappropriate, and that the task was to provide knowledge about the variety of human religious experience. "Religious Knowledge" in turn became "Religious Education", recognising the importance of students' own implicit religious experience and questioning which often did not fit a particular tradition.

Growing realisation of this failure to do justice to any religious tradition led to a phenomenological approach which attempted to give glimpses of experience from within. This failed, largely due to the marginalisation of the subject both within the school timetable and by government parsimony. The increasing tensions of a pluralistic society led almost full-circle back to Religious Studies, and the problems of the superficial knowledge of a wide variety of religious symbols, customs, and festivals, with little real encounter.

I was fortunate in two head teachers (one Quaker, one not) who encouraged me in grounding my work firmly in the lives and experience of our students. Describing our policy at the Quaker School to which I had moved, I wrote: "the Religious Education Department has attempted, within the constraints of traditional school time-table, hierarchy and structure, a 'person-centred' curriculum." We saw our roles as teachers as being enabler, facilitator, and co-learner. Students had rich opportunities for self-directed work, individually, in small groups and in class groups. "Goal-setting" and "priority" exercises featured regularly, as did self-assessment for review and evaluation and as a basis for the required end of term reports. One younger student graphically wrote "You're not a proper teacher - you're a human being!"

The arrival of a more traditional head-teacher made this emphasis problematic. I recall one group asking as we engaged in a lively role-play, "What will happen if the head teacher walks in?" So we role-played that too! Illuminating! A close friend and colleague described us as "the department of uncomfortable questions"! Pressures for a more traditional content-centred objective-based curriculum became strong.

Towards the end of my 18 years teaching there, to evaluate our work I undertook an "action research" project based at York University. My 1988 thesis was entitled "Towards an Inner Dimension of Teaching and Learning". In it I wrote of a growing groundswell seeking a rediscovery of a spiritual dimension in teaching and learning in all schools. This included techniques of relaxation; inward dialoguing through visualization and fantasy; the exploration of parable, riddles, spiritual folk-stories and wisdom tales; simple "attention" meditation; respecting and valuing the unique giftedness of life stories of students; and the teacher's willingness to be open to and share their own spiritual journeying.

Whilst the Quaker world provided the locus of my work and experience for over 20 years, my own sources of spiritual nourishment and exploration were mostly elsewhere. Early in my teaching career I was deeply influenced by the person-centered approach of Carl Rogers, powerfully supported by John Macmurray's radical challenges to our dualistic Cartesian thinking. The essence of our experience is to be found in relationships rather than in abstractions and objects, and the paradox of contradiction lies at the heart of all knowing.

My students introduced me to the poetry of Leonard Cohen and e.e.cummings. I thrived on the writings of people like Annie Dillard (*Pilgrim at Tinker Creek*) and Russell Hoban (*Teaching a Stone to Talk*). I revelled in the education conferences of the Dartington Trust, with their strong non-sectarian and inclusive spiritual dimension. There I encountered people like physicist David Bohm, biologist Rupert Sheldrake, and world pilgrim Satish Kumar. I drank in the spirit of the Findhorn community in northern Scotland. I met the despair and empowerment work of Joanna Macy, and became involved in her deep ecology work. I was inspired by Matthew Fox's "creation spirituality". These latter three came together in a remarkable week in April 1991 where we experienced the universality of the story and symbolism of Easter enacted through the dramas of Christian, Jewish, Buddhist, and pagan tradition.

I moved out of the classroom to work with other teachers; with Friends' programmes developing an ethos of partnership and participation in working with children and young people; with the Quaker Networks Project; and with the Northern Friends' Peace Board. After a period at Woodbrooke I came to Australia. Here I have had the valuable opportunity for further reflection and writing, including an in-depth study of the understanding of pastoral care amongst Friends, whilst tutoring in a Baptist College. I was also deeply involved in the development of a spiritual formation programme for Australian Quakers. I draw on a personal wealth of reflective writing from my studies and my journal writing as I assess my own growing understanding of whatever I mean by "God". Questions, rather than answers, are still central, as in Rainer Maria Rilke's letter to a young poet:

Be patient towards all that is unsolved in your heart.
Try to love the questions themselves.

Do not now seek answers that cannot be given
because you would not be able to live them,
And the point is to live everything.

Live the questions now.
Perhaps you will then gradually, without noticing it
Live along some distant day into the answers.

God?

Looking back, I was rarely comfortable with the way in which most people used the word "God". My few years of attachment to the Methodist and Anglican churches almost seem an aberration - though there was much that I learned, and value. I found release and comfort (even absolution!) in the "death of God" theology of the 1960s - typified for me by Werner and Lotte Pelz's *God is No More*. My own response was to use the "G" word as little as possible, preferring Paul Tillich's "ground of all being", "ultimate reality", or later the unpronounceable "God/ess" of some feminist writers, or even simply " "! The latter seemed to me in keeping with the traditional Jewish prohibition on pronouncing the divine YHWH, with the answer to Moses' question at the burning bush,"I am who I am", with Meister Eckhart's "Let go and let God be God", and with the Muslim abhorrence of imagery. It accords with the Quaker tradition in which I still find my own home, with the emphasis on the light within, and that of God within each individual. George Fox wrote in his *Journal* of "that Light and Spirit which was before the Scriptures were given forth, and which led the holy men of God to give them forth, that all might come to that Spirit if they would know God".

Yet, whilst for many years I have avoided the use of the "G" word, in Quaker circles I have found myself defending and making space for those who are at home with traditional theistic or Christian language, and who felt marginalised by its absence.

I find it instructive to look at the images, metaphors and symbols we use when speaking of g-d. At the age of seven, asked to respond to the Lord's Prayer with a picture, I drew a large gold-lined dark cloud with the sun's rays spreading forth from it. What was I saying about g-d, about my seven-year-old spirituality? At the age of 56 I took part in a walking meditation at Woodbrooke: walking three paces to each out-breath, my self-chosen mantra was "Mother earth"; three paces to each in-breath, "Nourish me". What was I saying about the earth, about "g-d"? About the same time I wrote in my personal journal:

Diving deeper - ever inwards
seeking and finding the living water
the flowing turbulent and steady river of life...
muddy and clear...
falling and flowing...

What was I now saying about my picture of "god"? about my spirituality?

I recall Gerry Hughes writing of a time walking on the slopes of Ben Lomond in Scotland, when for him "every bush was a burning bush". For me, Moses and Gerry Hughes were not imaging God, but telling of their responses to a sense of presence. How we describe that sense of presence is one thing, how we attempt to define it is another.

Is it "g-d"? In monotheistic traditions the symbol of God tends to be the primary symbol for the whole religious system and spiritual framework. For me, and for many at this time "g-d" remains an unnecessary term. The stories we have been told shape our experience, and our experience shapes the stories we tell. In the challenge of George Fox, so familiar to Friends: "You will say Christ saith this, and the apostles say this, but what canst thou say?" And this essay is my response.

In the 1970s BBC tv series *The Long Search* Ronald Eyre described an imagined conversation with a friend:

"Do you believe in God?"
"I'd rather not answer your question!"
The friend persists, "Do you believe in God?"
"I'd still rather not answer your question - and you won't understand if I do answer!"
"I'll try to understand - do you believe in God?"
"Yes!"

If this seems paradoxical and perverse, then so be it! The problem lies at the heart of traditional western philosophy and science. The Cartesian "cogito, ergo sum" [I think, therefore I am] places the emphasis on thought, rationality, and a logic which abhors contradiction. I've noted John Macmurray's alternative, "ago, ergo sum" [I act, therefore I am] with the emphasis on relationship and action. He suggests that any approach to truth must hold together opposites, like the two poles of a magnet, the two sides of a coin.

Sam Keen puts it succinctly and strongly (*Hymns to an Unknown God*, Bantam, New York, 1994):

Over the last century, the one solid truth established by psychologists is that the human psyche is constructed out of opposition, contradiction, and paradox. In problems of logic contradictory statements cannot be true; in the psyche only contradiction is true.

In various areas of contemporary science, something very similar holds: that a complete and whole description often requires that we use a variety of apparently contradictory images and metaphors. Perhaps paradox is at the heart of all being, at the heart of the universe.

Metaphor and symbol

If, as some claim, the symbol of God functions as the primary symbol for our whole religious system, what indeed is that symbol? All-powerful, all knowing-creator of the universe? - and this small part of the universe, mother earth, is ridden with conflict, violence, and destruction wrought by the supposedly most evolved creature of that creation! Is it surprising that this sounds like large chunks of the sacred scriptures of Jews and Christians? Lucy Goodison has commented "Monotheism is imperialism"! James

Hillman has noted, "We've had a hundred years of psychotherapy, and the world's getting worse"! What has been the impact of 1900 years of mainstream Christianity?

There are alternatives. Matthew Fox in his writings on creation spirituality challenges the assumptions of a fallen, sinful humanity, offering *original blessing* instead of *original sin*. The concept of a feminine wisdom spirit, Sophia, is strong in Jewish and Christian traditions, if largely hidden under the dominant patriarchal and androcentric mainstream (of all colours in the Christian spectrum). Sallie McFague, from her deep study of metaphorical theology, offers the image of the world as the body of God (*The Body of God: an Ecological Theology*, SCM Press, London, 1993). Other images are of God as mother, lover, and friend - all to be found in both biblical tradition and the writing of Christian mystics.

Early Quakers spoke of their faith as an "experimental" religion, firmly grounded in direct experience. In Britain Yearly Meeting's *Quaker Faith and Practice* the dominant metaphors for God are those of love, truth, light, depth, and the infinite.

Underlying our preferred symbols and metaphors lie a variety of world-views that permeate our thinking. Joanna Macy (deeply influenced by Buddhist tradition) challenges us in *World as Lover, World as Self* (Parallax Press, Berkely,1991). "How do we see our world? As a *battlefield*, in which we must seek to overcome evil, and all who oppose us? As a *classroom* where we are prepared for a future life? As a *trap* from which we must extricate or untangle ourselves before we can move on to higher things?" In each case, the world is seen as a proving ground with little inherent value of its own! "Or do we view the world as *our intimate and gratifying lover*? Or, more intimate still, as *a larger self*?" Each cell in the fingers I use to write this is made up of atoms that go back to the beginnings of space and time. In the palm of my hand are atoms that once roamed the planet in the feet of a dinosaur, or the wrigglings of an amoeba.

Can we any longer see ourselves as separate skin-encapsulated egos - a notion that Gregory Bateson once described as "the greatest epistemological fallacy of our time!"

Can we hear Thich Nhat Hanh's love-song (in *Complete Poems of Thich Nhat Hanh*, Parallax Press, 1992)?

Being rock, being gas, being mist, being Mind,
Being the mesons traveling among the galaxies with the speed of light,
You have come here, my beloved one.
You have manifested yourself as trees, as grass, as butterflies,
As single-celled beings and as chrysanthemums;
But the eyes with which you looked at me this morning
Tell me you have never died.

And if with Sallie McFague we see the world as the body of God, what then? But then perhaps "g-d" as word becomes superfluous - or as in the prologue of John's gospel, Word?

Each of these metaphors, images, world views can be found in almost all religious traditions, often pushed to the margins, even declared heretical.

Human-made language

Some 20 years ago I wrote:

Words: ships in the dark,
seeing the lights
failing to discern the shape
Radio messages - imposed on neural carrier waves
Coded with meaning
cold electromagnetic vibrations,
no warmth - no feeling - no touching
impartial - impersonal - open to all

Words - reaching, struggling,
attempting to create - unseeing
searching, questing,
missing the WORD
with cold formality

In my personal writing I struggle with the inadequacy of words available to me, wanting to combine shades of two (sometimes more) different words. Gender inclusivity may be a problem mostly forgotten, though I still shudder at the androcentrism of some writing. But the language I use is still an abstraction, the map is never the territory.

We cannot, like Humpty-Dumpty in *Alice in Wonderland*, make words mean whatever we wish them to mean! Nor is it just that, with T.S.Eliot,

words strain,
Crack and sometimes break under the burden,
Under the tension, slip, slide, perish,
Decay with imprecision, will not stay in place
Will not stay still

There are ways in which I am more deeply conditioned and formed by the language I use than ever I realise. We have, like Papunehang in his encounter with John Woolman, "to hear where words come from".

David Abrams (*The Spell of the Sensuous: Perception and Language in a More-Than-Human World*, Pantheon, New York, 1996) reminds us that the ancient Hebrew culture was the first in history to develop a truly *alphabetic* script. The gradual abandonment of carved symbols, pictograms and ideograms led to the development of a phonetic alphabet in the Semitic languages, further refined through the Greco-Roman civilisations and the Arabic world. And from the written word to the printed, and now the profusion and phantasmagoria of the electronic word, so we ever distance ourselves from embodied sensual experience!

Where indeed do words come from? How different is it to write this sitting at the computer keyboard from feeling my pen moving smoothly and rhythmically on paper? And how much more different from the experience of lying under the night sky immersed in the immensity of the star-filled cosmos?

When one compares our complex developed printed language with that of many indigenous peoples, the effect on our consciousness becomes clearer still. Perhaps the combination of alphabetic abstraction with western dualism and rationalism overwhelms us. Does the language I use say more about me than about the object or experience or abstraction I seek to describe?

Rupert Ross, in his exploration of North American aboriginal languages (*Return to the Teachings: Exploring Aboriginal Justice*, Penguin, 1996), shows clearly how judgmental, abstract, and object (noun) oriented English is. Try spending even a few minutes not using any nouns or adjectives in your conversation! Sakej Henderson (Director of the Native Law Centre,

University of Saskatoon) has said that when talking in, say, Mikmaq, he could talk all day long and never utter a single noun. "For some reason, English speakers seem to have chosen to live under the rule of King Noun. We Aboriginal people would rather think of ourselves as being in bed with Queen Verb."

Questing still

I am reminded of Philip Rack's paragraphs (in Britain YM *Quaker Faith and Practice*, 20.06) about the difference between living on the rocks of certainty or in the surf of the unknown.

Some among us have a reassuring certitude and steadiness which can serve as a reference point by which others may navigate. There are others who live in a state of uncertainty, constantly re-thinking their responses to changing circumstances, trying to hold onto what seems fundamental but impelled to reinterpret, often even unsure where lies the boundary between the fundamental and the interpretation...

Please be patient, those of you who have found a rock to stand on, with those of us who haven't and with those of us who are not even looking for one. We live on the wave's edge, where sea, sand and sky are all mixed up together: we are tossed head over heels in the surf, catching only occasional glimpses of any fixed horizon. Some of us stay there from choice because it is exciting and it feels like the right place to be.

Is this the same as John Keats' "negative capability" where he describes the person of achievement as "capable of being in uncertainties, mysteries, doubts, without any irritable reaching after fact and reason"? Krishnamurti suggests that it is in such times of uncertainty that our deepest creativity flourishes.

As contemporary chaos theorists remind us, we are part of a vast interconnected process, unfinished, evolving. We cannot know or even envision what order, or disorder the future holds. Perhaps that is why, so often, I have to turn to the poet to give adequate expression to my quest. So often, as with Janet Kalven in *Respectable Outlaw*, it is still as if I

have set sail on another ocean,
without star or compass,
going where the argument leads,
shattering the certainties
of centuries.

★ ★ ★

Sandy Parker *is a member of Geelong Meeting, Victoria, Australia, and was clerk of Victoria Regional Meeting 2002-5.*

Further reading: John Briggs and David Peat, "Seven Life Lessons in Chaos: Timeless Wisdom for the Science of Change", Harper Collins, NY, 1998.

Listening to the Kingdom

Bowen Alpern

Held to the standard of being an effective midwife for the Kingdom of God, the Religious Society of Friends appears stuck, demoralized, and emaciated. So much so that it would not occur to most Friends that we could be held to such a standard.

Nontheism as method

Experience ossifies automatically, inexorably, tragically, into concept. Any experience: eating warm cherry pie, falling in love, driving into a tree. The process occurs on both the individual and the societal levels. It applies with particular poignancy to those experiences people tend to classify as "religious".

This presents a problem to any religion. Concepts become dead forms lacking power. The religion loses its ability to speak to the real conditions of people, becoming a mere mechanism for social control. Full of passion perhaps, but without life, without the power to transform and liberate.

The inverse process of recovering the experience behind a concept is haphazard, fragile, never completely satisfying. A blade of grass will find a way up through the asphalt. Someone will stumble onto an experience that breathes new life into old concepts. If that someone is good and strong and brave, new truth speaks to the condition of many. She becomes a threat to those who manipulate the old religion. Martyrdom cauterizes the wound to the social order, but leaves a new religion, or a renewed old one, in its wake. The cycle begins anew.

The process by which experience devolves into concept poses a unique challenge to the Religious Society of Friends, because it is intrinsically a religion of experience. This experience must be kept alive for the Society to continue. But, the only way experience is "kept alive" is as concept, and concept just isn't good enough. Quakerism cannot be taught; each Quaker must reinvent it for herself. However, it is not re-experienced in a vacuum, but in dialogue with other Quakers, living and dead.

In an invited message given to Southern Appalachian Yearly Meeting and Association in 2003 (in a wonderful new collection *Wrestling with Our Faith*

Tradition, Quaker Press of Friends General Conference), Lloyd Lee Wilson identifies this process as wrestling with Quaker tradition. His reference is to the story of Isaac wrestling all night with an angel and making it bless him. In wrestling with tradition, one is transformed by it. And, usually to a much lesser extent, the tradition is transformed as well. It remains alive.

This is a beautifully democratic vision of what the doing of religion is. One does not have to surrender whatever shreds remain of one's integrity to begin the process. One starts where one finds oneself. This is an inviting vision for a nontheist. Although she may suspect that the theist expects her to find God in the end, the expectation need not be normative. All that is required is that she wrestle honestly. Well and good, but how precisely can a nontheist wrestle honestly with a tradition so mired in the language of God?

My thesis is that nontheism itself provides a method. Since the nontheist does not believe in God, she cannot take those aspects of the tradition that are expressed in God language at face value. Instead, she chooses to assume that these expressions reflect, in some distorted way, an important underlying experience. She further chooses to assume that it may be possible to revive that experience by groping for a way of re-expressing it without mentioning God.

The nontheist is aware that neither of these assumptions may be valid. It is possible that any particular religious concept may be based entirely on bigotry, prejudice, superstition, or pure drivel and utterly without any socially redeeming content. On the other hand, it may be that the experience behind the concept is quite real and transcendently important but absolutely unintelligible without God talk.

The nontheist need not expect that a successful redescription of any particular concept can be easily achieved. She merely stands in the possibilities provided by her assumptions, and waits, as expectantly as possible, for ways to open. This is her method.

My hunch is that by systematically, skillfully, imaginatively, and faithfully applying this method the nontheist may be able to gain insight that can be of value even to theists. Suffice it to say that I am not there yet. Still, this essay aspires to "do Quakerism" from a nontheist perspective, attempting a prophetic examination of the current condition of, and immediate prospects for, the Religious Society of Friends.

A culture of invidious comparison

Friends are, in general, rightly proud of our heritage. Mingled with that pride is an uneasiness. There is a palpable sense that modern Friends are not living up to the example of our forebears - that we are not as pious in our worship or as upright in our witness. Consequently, our accomplishments cannot be expected to stand up to theirs. This sensibility is almost ubiquitous among Friends. And, for that reason, it is invisible; we take it for granted.

Some observations about this sensibility are in order. First, it may or may not be warranted. It could be argued that each generation of Friends has been more insipid than the one that preceded it until all we are now left with is good feelings and hot air. However, it is at least plausible that living Friends are embarking, or are about to embark, upon a series of projects that will far overshadow all that dead Friends have achieved.

This sensibility is suspiciously consistent with a more general nostalgia satirized in the Louis Malle film *Atlantic City*. In one scene, an ageing gangster describes to a young protégé how much better the old days were. He ends up saying that when he was young the Atlantic was a *real* ocean. People have been saying that the world is going to hell in a hand basket since the invention of the hand basket.

The culture of invidious comparison is *not* a new phenomenon among Friends. Almost from the beginning, Quakers have seen themselves and their contemporaries as failing to measure up to the standard of earlier Friends. This sentiment can be found in *The Journal of John Woolman* and in the writings of his contemporaries. Most of what Friends now take pride in is itself a product of this culture. Indeed, it may be that this sensibility has spurred some Friends to greater efforts in an attempt to live up to their predecessors.

Much of what we tend to regard as the achievement of Friends as a whole was, in fact, the work of individual Friends, or small groups of Friends, often in the face of opposition or neglect from their monthly meetings. (One of the most positive - if often tedious - aspects of Quaker culture may be its capacity to produce or attract individuals who are willing to stand up to it.)

Finally, it seems highly unlikely that the effects of this sensibility have been, or are, uniformly beneficial. One might speculate, for example, on the role it may have played in the various separations that have plagued our Society.

A brief history of Friends

Any attempt to assess the current state of the Religious Society of Friends needs to take this culture of invidious comparison into account. It is not hard to see how it developed. The Quaker movement exploded onto interregnum England shaking the foundations of an already shaky society. Early Friends proclaimed that Christ had risen *in them* and was rising *in the world*. These first Quakers saw an intrinsic connection between the mundane choices of their daily lives and the realization of the Kingdom of God on earth. This connection both transformed their lives and infused those lives with power. This millenarian movement quickly came to be perceived as a threat by vested interests in Cromwell's Protectorate.

An observer gave fear of an "armed Quaker uprising" as one reason for the restoration of Charles II. With restoration came persecution. Friends reacted heroically, defiantly continuing to practice their proscribed faith openly, incurring much suffering in the process. At the same time, Quakerism shed much of its revolutionary character. A modified Presbyterian system of hierarchical monthly, regional, and yearly meetings was imposed to exert social control over wayward Friends. The Kingdom was postponed.

The origin of the culture of invidious comparison can be precisely dated to May 1689 and the passage of the Toleration Act. From that point on, things got easier. Quakers became rich - in part because the poor could not afford to remain Friends. To survive, the poor relied in countless petty ways upon the meager generosity of the rich, who exacted a very unQuakerly deference in return. Discouraged from careers in the military, the church and politics by a mixture of scruple and law, English Friends concentrated on industry and commerce, where their frugal lifestyle, their reputation for honesty, their refusal to bargain, and their emerging transatlantic connections contributed to success. Not all Friends were successful, but the unsuccessful played little part in running the Society (bankruptcy meant disownment). In their material comfort, later generations of Quakers looked back, and still look back, on the first generation of Friends with an awe often tinged with guilt.

In the quietist period, the Quaker meeting was run by a triumvirate of ministers, elders, and overseers. Over time this structure ossified. A pietistic reform movement (Woolman, Scott, Hicks, etc.) tried to reground American

Quakerism in the direct experience of the divine. This movement was intuitively understood by the triumvirs as a threat to their power and material comfort. (Just how easy is it for the rich to enter the Kingdom?). They responded with a counter-reformation that subordinated individual experience to the authority of the historical Jesus and the Bible. This transformed what Howard Brinton has called a fourth branch of Christianity - distinct from the Eastern Orthodox, Catholics, and Protestants - into another Protestant sect.

Modernist Quakerism in America

In the wake of this transformation, American Quakerism fractured into Orthodox and Hicksite branches. The Conservative branch later split off from the Orthodox, trying to maintain the old quietist structure. Among the Hicksites, Lucretia Mott and her fellow radicals concluded that the old structure was untenable and proceeded to dismantle it. This process required most of a century.

Meanwhile, the Orthodox were experiencing unprecedented growth and careening toward an extreme fundamentalism. To deal with the growth, the pastoral system evolved, largely eclipsing the triumvirate. In reaction to the fundamentalism, a reform movement crystallizing around people such as John Wilhelm Rowntree, Rufus Jones, and Hannah and Joel Bean, brought a significant part of the Orthodox tradition closer to the Hicksites.

By the middle of the twentieth century American Quakerism was pretty much polarized between fundamentalist Orthodox yearly meetings in the Midwest and West and modernist yearly meetings (nominally Hicksite, Orthodox, or independent) on the East and West Coasts, with a few Conservative Yearly Meetings seemingly fading away. Within a few years, all of the co-located Hicksite and Orthodox yearly meetings on the East Coast had reunited. In modern liberal Quakerism, the triumvirate survived, if at all, in vestigial form, largely replaced by standing committees, conferences, and worship-sharing. All Friends were ministers and "eldering" had become a bad word.

Although the 1960s represent a cultural high-water mark for the Quaker values of non-violence, equality, integrity, and simplicity, by the end of the Vietnam war modernist Quakerism had entered a crisis that persists to this day. Social Gospel Protestantism had proved impotent against the demonic power of racism, militarism, and corporate greed. The beloved community theology of the early civil rights movement had morphed into the separatism of Black Power. The antiwar movement had itself turned to violence. Global capitalism ran unfettered and amuck. Dreams of a better world died hard.

Internally, the ossification of modernist Quakerism became apparent. The term "Yearly Meeting Friends" signified a divide between those with the leisure, resources, and commitment to be active in wider Quaker bodies and those who participated only in their monthly meeting. The system of standing committees became bureaucratic. Nominating committees "filled slots" more often than they "recognized gifts". The connection between worship and witness became strained. By the late 1980s, Friends in New York Yearly Meeting had turned on each other. The larger society's culture wars played out on the floor of the yearly meeting. Attendance stagnated; membership declined.

Postmodern Quakerism

From this parched ground, new life springs. I will call out a few instances. There are no doubt others.

Probably least important is the phenomenon of open and interconnected *nontheist* Friends. Ten years of workshops at Friends General Conference (FGC) Gathering, Pendle Hill, and Woodbrooke (resulting in a vigorous online discussion) have created a global community of Friends exploring what it might mean to try to live a religious life without God, insisting on being honest about what they do and do not believe. And now these Friends are coming out with an anthology. The emergence of this tendency might potentially open up the prospect of a truly universal church that has been closed for centuries.

The Alternatives to Violence Program began as a collaboration between predominantly African-American inmates in the New York prison system and mostly European-American Quakers in New York Yearly Meeting as an effort to curb youth violence. It has spread throughout the world, being used, for instance, in the aftermath of genocide in Rwanda. The seeds of this collaboration across divides of race and class are just beginning to flower within New York Yearly Meeting.

The community of Lesbian, Gay, Bisexual, Transgendered, and Queer

Friends has been an amazing source of spiritual vitality for the Religious Society of Friends. This community has transformed the pain of social ostracism and the grief of AIDS into a powerful witness. Its open meeting for worship is the heart of FGC Gatherings. Its presence among Friends is a vivid illustration of how diversity might yet appear in areas where it is profoundly lacking.

Finally, there is a tendency that seeks to renew modernist Quakerism by recovering quietist Quaker forms, institutions, and insights, which finds expression in Lloyd Lee Wilson's first book *Essays on the Quaker Vision of Gospel Order*, FGC's Traveling Ministries Program, the School of the Spirit, the *Quaker Ranter* blog, etc.. New (or perhaps old) meaning is being discovered for such classic Quaker terms as minister, elder, gifts of the Spirit, and gospel order. It might be called "neo-Conservative," if the term had not been pre-empted. While this trend sometimes appears blissfully ignorant of the struggles that led to abandoning earlier forms, we would be wrong to dismiss it as merely reactionary. It does not seek to impose the past on the present, but rather to salvage from the past artifacts that can be refashioned to empower spiritual life in the contemporary world. It is typically postmodern.

Wrestling with neo-traditional Quakerism

It is difficult, but perhaps important, for nontheist Friends to engage with this tendency. At the core of the difficulty is the neo-traditionalist insistence on the primacy of the relationship of the individual with God - an insistence that goes back to early Friends.

However difficult, neo-traditionalists hold out a vision of a way of living that I find in some ways compelling. It is a vision of a life freed up, not from desire, but from the thralldom of desire; not from self, but from the centrality of self. It's the kind of life one might imagine Leon Trotsky living as he charged into battle rallying a faltering Red Army with the cry "Trotsky is with you". (There are reasons one might want to subject such lives to the discipline of a pacifist faith community.)

Clearly, such a life requires a surrender of will, or an ongoing attempt at such surrender. But, to whom or what? A multitude of candidates present themselves: the proletarian revolution, one's country, any number of leaders or would-be leaders both secular and religious. One shudders in disgust at most of them. The Christian candidate is Christ. This is somewhat vague, and, to the nontheist, more than a little suspect: whose idea of Christ? The history of Christianity has not been entirely pretty.

The neo-traditionalist answers "your own *experience* of Christ as tested with your faith community". This is somewhat reassuring but also somewhat slippery. To hope to live every moment under the direction of the Holy Spirit, one is asked to accept a story about an infallible, omnipotent, loving God and a victory achieved on a cross in the deep past that is certain but yet to be realized, etc., and to find one's place in this bigger story of God's unfolding love.

I suspect that, even for many theists, this story is no longer credible. (To say nothing of those for whom the very idea of God after Auschwitz is blasphemy). I, for one, am not interested in the promise of a new life based on this kind of certainty (or on any other kind of certainty for that matter). But can one live a transformed life grounded only in uncertainty and doubt? This is the real challenge the neo-traditionalist poses to the nontheist!

The question remains open. I can only testify that it is possible to try, or at least to try to try. If one is prepared to make such a commitment, the work of the neo-traditionalists can be of value.

Instead of striving for a direct relationship with God, might one not try to be faithful to her Kingdom? If, as Lloyd Lee Wilson insists, it is necessary to find one's place in a story bigger than oneself, doesn't the age-old struggle of humankind to lift itself out of the muck of selfishness, exploitation, and violence, and to create the Peaceable Kingdom - the socialist commonwealth, the republic of virtue, the promised land, a world without unnecessary suffering, where people are motivated by love and self-expression rather than fear and greed - provide just such a story? The story of a shining city silently entreating every human heart "Build me! Build me, *now*!"

Part of me wants to get swallowed up in that story. It promises to answer my deepest hungers. And yet, there is a part of me that recoils, pleading the price is too high, knowing that that price is its own death.

This is a dicey business of course. Much of the world's madness is done in the name of God and her Kingdom. One needs to honor one's hesitances, even while striving to overcome them. The discernment of a supportive faith community seems requisite.

Besides, we have been cheated too often. After untold centuries of carnage and disappointment, this Kingdom is even less credible than God herself. For some, it is a shadow-puppet used to manipulate the gullible. For many, it is an empty cipher, another hollow abstraction.

It will be objected that the Kingdom is not some utopia to be postponed into an indefinite future, but an alternative reality that you and I can experience in the present moment. I am increasingly convinced that the Kingdom of God must be understood dialectically. The thesis - the Kingdom of Genesis - is that the world as it is, warts and all, is perfect. This understanding contains within it its antithesis - the Kingdom of the Prophets - the conviction that the world is far from perfect. The synthesis - the Kingdom of the historical Jesus - is implicit in his saying "the Kingdom of God is / will presently be within / among you." (The ambiguities appear intentional). This Kingdom is available to each of us as we give up our lives to the process which transforms the-world-as-it-is into the-world-as-it-ought-to-be.

Whether it is possible to transcend selfishness completely without abandoning ourselves to God, I cannot say. However, in my experience, it is sometimes possible to find a kind of clearness where my desires, even when strongly held, are seen as neither bad nor good, but merely irrelevant to the choice at hand. Perhaps this is enough.

What's past is prelude

Returning to the current state of Quakerism, is it possible to gain some mastery over our culture of invidious comparison? Can't we tell our story in a way that casts the accomplishments of the past as preparation for work to be done in our time?

We could begin by measuring the accomplishments of previous generations of Friends, not in absolute terms, but against the cultural opening that their historical moment presented to them - not that the scope of such openings can be gauged with any kind of accuracy.

Still, from this angle, the astounding achievement of the first generation of Friends is less daunting. They had an enormous opening to play in. The king - who, the common people had been taught by their "betters," ruled by divine right - had just been executed by those "betters" for treason against the commonwealth. Hopes rose, but attempts at further reform were crushed.

The king had been defeated, but the "kingly power" had not. Quakers identified the cause of the betrayal as "sin," in particular, the pride, acquisitiveness, and lusts of those "betters". The Fall of Adam was understood as the justification for clothing, government, social hierarchy, private property, and the subjugation of women. Quakers preached perfection and "went naked for a sign".

Preaching perfection, it was necessary to practise it. At that turbulent moment it was just possible to believe that the Kingdom might well be at hand and that the mundane actions of one's daily life could make the difference. Christ has risen *in me* and will rise *in the world,* not in some distant future but in my lifetime. Millennial hope proved a powerful incentive to personal rectitude.

But, that hope failed. No subsequent generation of Friends has been given an opening comparable to that of the first generation. Furthermore, that generation exhausted a possibility: is Christ still risen? If so, how many more generations will his victory take? If not, and he were to rise tomorrow, would that be a *Third* Coming? Quaker millenarianism is no longer a viable option.

What is to be done?

No generation of Quakers has faced an opening comparable to that given early Friends. Except perhaps our own! Granted, the opening we find ourselves in feels very narrow indeed. It seems as though not only the poor but racism, war, and the gluttonous waste of scarce resources will always be with us. But this feeling is the direct product of the world's relentless insistence that nothing will make a difference, that our lives don't matter. Part of the job of religion is to create a safe place where that voice can be ignored and the Truth of an unknown future can be faced in fear and trembling.

A year before his assassination, Dr. Martin Luther King Jr. issued a call for a "radical revolution of values" to exorcise the demons of "racism, materialism, and militarism" at the core of American culture. Against each of these demons, Friends maintain a venerable testimony: equality, simplicity, and peace.

This revolution is now forty years overdue. America's slide toward "spiritual death" proceeds. The Republic transforms into Empire before our eyes.

Politicians have learned to manipulate the addiction of the American people to war - "the force that gives us meaning" - to win elections. Child sacrifice, and the attendant vicarious grief at the deaths of young American solders, is a sacrament in the dominant religion in the United States: the cult of redemptive violence. Racism festers. Environmental catastrophe looms on multiple fronts. It may well be too late, but this is not certain.

Nothing is certain. But, there are growing signs the status quo cannot hold much longer. The rest of the world is drawn inexorably into a coalition to oppose the Empire. Americans seem to be turning against this particular war at least. A burning rage at the systemic racism, inequality, and environmental degradation incumbent in our capitalist economy roils somewhere beneath the surface of American life. There is a growing awareness that something has been going horribly wrong in America for a long time. All hell may break loose!

9/11 and its aftermath have not resolved the crisis of modernist Quakerism, but have further cemented a fragile unity that was beginning to crystallize before the first plane struck. The focus has shifted from internal to external. Slowly, hesitantly, tentatively, American Quakerism reorients itself against the Empire.

Quakers cannot fight Martin King's revolution alone. Neither are we apt to lead it. We are, however, uniquely fitted to *ground* it - to demonstrate the connection between the change we want in the world and how we live our daily lives. Although Quaker culture understands the imperative for such grounding - it is our testimony of integrity - we have difficulty putting theory into practice. However, even our failure to live up to our values can become a source of strength. It can teach us humility and compassion for our compatriots as we all struggle to throw off our corporate addiction to mass violence.

Becoming whole

To carry out this witness faithfully, the Religious Society of Friends must become whole. It must transcend theological, generational, and racial divides to which we have become unconsciously accustomed. To do this, it will need to grow, probably faster and more recklessly, than most Friends will be comfortable with.

To become whole, we must regard theological differences as a source of strength. We must value shared commitment above shared belief. We must reach out to those whose beliefs frighten us. We must abandon our fruitless but addictive striving after orthodoxy for the real work of seeking a viable orthopraxy.

To become whole, we must fill in the gap between Friends under eighteen and Friends over fifty. It will not be enough to attract and make comfortable the young adults in our meetings. We must learn to speak to their spiritual needs, and to recognize and nurture their spiritual gifts. We don't do this very well in general.

To become whole, North American Quakerism must lose its racial homogeneity. White Friends will need to do the hard work of routing out the unconsciously internalized attitudes of a racist society. But, this will not be enough!

It seems plausible to me that the natural complexion of our Society, at least in North America, would be something like thirty to fifty percent people of color, perhaps more. This is a rough guess based on my sense of the relative proportions of various groups in the general population whose values are basically in tune with our testimonies, who are reasonably tolerant of theological diversity, who are open to the possibility of nonhierarchical prophetic ministry, who could learn to sit in expectant waiting, and who would be willing to make group decisions by "sense of the meeting".

Becoming whole will entail finding ways of achieving our natural complexion, whatever this turns out to be. This will require drawing nonwhite people into almost all-white meetings. It may also mean creating new meetings composed largely of people who are not white. This will necessitate finding ways to equip meetings where most of the membership is relatively new to Friends. Quakers have dealt with similar difficulties in the past, but the results were not always happy. Opportunities for racially tinged misunderstanding (if not worse) are staggering.

Beginning

The challenges are enormous. It seems far-fetched to suppose that the Religious Society of Friends we know and love could find the courage, skills, resources, and commitment to transform itself so radically. This is alright!

We cannot become whole just because we want to. If we are to become whole, it will be because the projects we engage in require it of us, dragging us to a place to which we could not otherwise come. It will take a miracle, many miracles.

We must start where we are. It is immoral to sacrifice for an abstraction, no matter how beautiful. We must take the baby steps that make sense in terms of the narrow opening in which we feel ourselves to be. We must learn to trust ourselves, each other, and the process evolving around us. Trust that, as the opening unfolds, we will find the strength and grace to dance with our commitments rather than our fears. Trust that, as we move hesitantly forward, others will find themselves caught up in our vision and contributing unimagined new vistas to it. Trust that resistance will beget fortitude and that fortitude will overcome resistance. Trust, finally, that the way we live our lives can make a difference in the world.

Can we allow ourselves to be transformed by the opportunity that stares back at us? Can we come to respond to conflicts in our meetings as gifts of the Spirit, laboratory exercises that can help us to make real our commitment to the possibility of peaceful reconciliation? It is not necessary that we resolve every conflict, only that we try, and when we fail, that we acknowledge it is we who have failed, and that we love one another.

Can we live our lives as if they matter?

It seems highly unlikely that we will end up with much to show for our efforts. We know we must let go of our attachment to results. But just perhaps, when someone sits down in 2152 to write *Friends for Five Hundred Years*, she will conclude that this was the greatest generation of Quakers.

Afterthought

George Fox would have been disgusted by this essay. He would not merely have disagreed with its logic and conclusions: he would have dismissed the whole project as misguided from its inception. "Notions!" he would have labeled it, a distraction from the real business of being still and experiencing the illumination available to each of us regardless of what we believe. We need not give George the final word of course, but it does seem a fruitful caution to bear in mind.

Bowen Alpern, *a self-described Jewish, Marxist, atheist, gospel minister of Christ, is a member of Scarsdale Friends Meeting of New York Yearly Meeting. He is, or has been, clerk of the Ministry & Worship committee of SFM and the Ministry & Counsel committee of Purchase Quarterly Meeting, and a member of the coordinating committee for Ministry & Counsel of NYYM, the Ministry & Nurture committee of Friends General Conference, and its ad hoc Youth Ministries Discernment committee. With his wife, Robin, and her father, Glenn Mallison, he co-led the "Nontheism Among Friends" workshop at the FGC Gathering in Hamilton, Ontario in 1996.*

The Making of a Quaker Nontheist Tradition

David Boulton and Os Cresson

Quaker nontheism in its current form was a twentieth century development. But it was not created from nothing. In this chapter David Boulton (on Gerrard Winstanley) and Os Cresson (on David Duncan, the Manchester radicals and Henry J Cadbury) recall some of the pioneers who opened the road to a naturalist or humanist interpretation of the Quaker tradition.

Gerrard Winstanley: Digger, True Leveller and Quaker

'In the beginning of time the great Creator Reason made the earth to be a common treasury.'

The "True Leveller" or "Digger" leader Gerrard Winstanley was one of the most radical religious and political thinkers in seventeenth century Britain. He was thought by many to be "the leader of the Quakers", and Thomas Comber, Dean of Durham, claimed in 1678 that George Fox's "cubs" derived their mischievous ideas from Winstanley's writings. In fact, all twenty of Winstanley's pamphlets and books were written in the four years from 1648 to 1652, and although he mixed with London Friends briefly in 1654 he did not become a Quaker until the 1670s when his name first appears in the registers of Westminster Monthly Meeting. We may guess that his outspoken nontheism, coupled with his advocacy of Christian communism, was a radicalism too far, even for the revolutionary young George Fox. But it may well be that Winstanley, like Fox, mellowed as he grew older, and perhaps by the 1670s they could meet in the middle, where Fox's "that of God in every man" and Winstanley's "God [or Reason] within" could negotiate a peaceful co-existence.

Winstanley was born in Wigan, Lancashire, in 1609. In or around 1630 he travelled south to London to be apprenticed to a merchant tailor, Sarah Gates, who was probably a kinswoman. She was the widow of a former puritan minister turned cloth merchant, and as well as having inherited her husband's business she had also come into possession of his well-stocked theological library. Lodging with her, as was usual with apprentices, young Gerrard probably picked up as much theology as tailoring skills. By 1637 he was a freeman of the Merchant Tailors Company and in 1640 he married Susan King, daughter of a small landowner in Cobham, Surrey.

The outbreak of civil war in 1642 hit his business hard. Within a year he was bankrupt. "I was beaten out both of estate and trade," he wrote, "and forced... to live a country life" - apparently as a grazier and cowherd on his father-in-law's smallholding. But this was a time of intense religious and political upheaval. King and court fought Parliament, the established Church of England siding with the Crown and breakaway dissenting churches lining up with Parliament. Winstanley, like Fox, became a seeker, turning from being "a strict goer to church" to "dipping" (the Baptists), and to one sect after another. Politically, he turned radical republican. In 1648, with King Charles defeated and facing execution, Winstanley suddenly produced three publications that instantly established him as an astonishingly original and inspirational thinker.

First, his message is uncompromisingly universalist: all shall be saved, the poor and the bad as well as the rich and the good. But salvation is to be understood metaphorically, as is all religious language. The Bible is man-made and not to be taken literally. The Devil is a symbol of human selfishness: "What you call the devil is within you". Heaven is not a place above the bright blue sky, but "the communion of saints is a true heaven". Angels? They are (as William Blake might have written a century and a half later) "the sparks of glory or heavenly principles set in men". The Day of Judgment is a metaphor, as is the resurrection of the dead. Even the Ten Commandments are rejected as a law to which the spirit is superior. And God? And Christ? It is the devil "which leads men to imagine God in a place of glory beyond the skies". God is neither an external being nor a deified historical Jesus. Christ "is not a single man at a distance from you but the indwelling power of reason".

So "you are not to be saved by believing that a man lived and died long ago at Jerusalem, but by the power of the spirit within you treading down all unrighteousness of the flesh. Neither are you to look for God in a place of glory beyond the sun, but within yourself and within every man... He that looks for a God outside himself, and worships God at a distance, worships he knows not what, but is... deceived by the imagination of his own heart."

What is this God, this spirit? "The Spirit or Father", says Winstanley, "is pure reason", the "spirit of right understanding" by which "man is called a reasonable creature, which is a name given to no other creature". "Let reason rule the man, and he dares not trespass against his fellow-creature, but will do as he would be done unto. For reason tells him, Is thy neighbour hungry and naked today, do thou feed and clothe him; it may be thy case tomorrow." Reason "knits every creature together into a oneness, making every creature to be an upholder of his fellow". Reason is "the Lord Christ" who "will spread himself in multiplicities of bodies, making them all of one heart and mind, acting in the righteousness one to another". But if reason is a wholly human creation, reason also created the human family: "In the beginning of time the great Creator Reason made the earth to be a common treasury..."

For Winstanley, the principle of reason and unselfishness urged that all distinction between rich and poor, haves and have-nots, was unnatural and abhorrent. Private property, particularly in unequal distribution, was a corruption of selfishness, the very devil. This led Winstanley to agitate for a form of Christian communism in which the land and its resources would be confiscated from private owners and turned over to local communities. The church had lost its power, the Lords had lost their seats (with the abolition of the House of Lords) and the king had lost his head in January 1649. In April that year Winstanley led his "Digger" comrades onto a patch of common land near his father-in-law's smallholding and began his experiment in collective farming. It lasted a year before it was violently broken up by a mob led by the local parson, magistrate and lord of the manor, John Platt. Winstanley wrote a final defiant manifesto for Christian communism, dedicated to Cromwell in 1652, before fading into obscurity.

Even as his manifesto hit the presses (it was printed by Giles Calvert, who would become the Quakers' publisher) another young agitator, George Fox, was stirring up radical Seekers in the moors and mountains of Westmorland to give the nascent Quaker movement lift-off. Two years later, when Francis Howgill and Edward Burrough exported the new northern religion to London, Winstanley came to their meetings and expressed the hope that the Quakers would pick up his work where he had been forced to leave off. In this he would be disappointed. Friends would be radical liberals rather than revolutionary socialists. But aspects of Winstanley's theology would take root among Friends, and Winstanley would become a Friend himself in his later years.

Winstanley despised supernaturalist religion, seeing at close quarters how it struck fear and anguish into the puritan soul. Mankind was "assaulted with this doctrine of a God, a Devil, a Heaven and a Hell, salvation and damnation after a man is dead... If the passion of sorrow predominate, then he is heavy and sad, crying out he is damned, God hath forsaken him and he must go to Hell when he dies, he cannot make his calling and election sure. And in that distemper many times a man doth hang, kill or drown himself: so that this divining doctrine which [the clergy] call 'spiritual and heavenly things', torments people...". True religious ministry dealt with "the nature of mankind, of his darkness and of his light, of his weakness and of his strength, of his love and of his envy, of his sorrow and his joy, of his inward and outward bondages, and of his inward and outward freedoms". It was what a man (or a woman: Winstanley more than any of his contemporaries went out of his way to include women, even if "inclusive language" had yet to be invented) "hath found out by his own industry and observation in trial".

As Cromwell had dethroned Charles I and proclaimed a republic of England, so Winstanley dethroned the heavenly king and preached a republic of heaven. Thus "Quaker nontheism" may be seen as dating back to the earliest infancy of the Quaker movement.

David Duncan and the Free Friends of Manchester

'Truth for authority, and not authority for truth'

In 1858, Friends in Manchester, England, opened an Institute next to their meetinghouse for their numerous young people who, having no other place to go, were gathering in taverns to debate the issues of the day.

It was an exciting time to be in Manchester. There was a college, an art school, and a Literary and Philosophical Society (where Joseph Priestley and John Dalton had been members). Manchester was a great textile manufacturing center and there was much radical agitation for reform. A local Friend, John Bright, was one of the leading orators and social reformers in Parliament.

It was also an exciting time to be a Friend, and a difficult one. Some restrictions were loosening and would soon disappear, such as requirements that Friends use plain clothes and speech, and only marry other Friends. The evangelical movement among Friends was in the ascendancy and elders in the meetings sought to control what Quakers said and wrote about their faith, which met with some resistance.

At the Manchester Friends' Institute 150 members talked about science, religion, art, politics and reform. They immersed themselves in the philosophy and politics of J S Mill and Guiseppi Mazzini, the essays and poetry of Woolman and Whittier, the aphorisms of Epictetus. They were known for boisterous exchanges and hard questioning and their speeches and writings drew the attention of the national Quaker press.

The little group included some extraordinary people. David Duncan was a linen merchant who had been a Presbyterian minister before marrying Sarah Ann Cooke, a Quaker. He was a clear thinker and writer, a sensitive and engaging person who was revered by younger members of the Institute. Duncan's parents, David and Fanny, lived near by. They came from Magherafelt, in Londonderry, Ireland. David and Sarah had six children whose later jobs were artist, governess, nurse, teacher and merchant.

Joseph Binyon Forster was a sugar refiner and planter who was a skilled editor. He and Mary Beakbane had five children, one of whom became an artist. Charles Thompson was a magistrate and city councilman. Mary Jane Hodgson was an artist and poet, and George Stewardson Brady was a physician and botanist, a Fellow of the Royal Society in London, and an outspoken defender of Charles Darwin.

This assembly of free thinkers questioned the divinity of Christ, the atonement and the divine inspiration of the Bible. Individual truth was tested by living with the truth and this they set over all other authority. Others saw this as an attempted revolution but they said it was simply returning to the ways of early Friends.

Their spirited defense of liberty did not include one element now common: we turn to the meeting community to test our personal leadings. Perhaps, at that time, this would have resulted in the meeting's reasserting doctrinal control. Also, it could have been seen as denying that the individual's light is sufficient. Today, a third way is possible in which the community provides a useful setting for discovering what one is called to do.

During the 1860s disputes broke out with Manchester Preparative Meeting over censorship of books and lectures. There was also disagreement over the suitability of one of their number who was in line to become clerk. Finally, after the radicals had pressed their views on a visiting minister, the elders took action. They selected David Duncan and charged him with heresy. The issue went to Hardshaw East Monthly Meeting and Lancaster and Cheshire Quarterly Meeting, and then London Yearly Meeting formed a committee to investigate, led by the renowned evangelical Friend Joseph Bevan Braithwaite.

The hearings turned into a contest between individual experience and established doctrine. Calls for moderation failed and separation became inevitable. David Duncan was expelled from membership in August 1871. His supporters immediately gathered in his home for worship. He could not attend, being ill with what turned out to be smallpox. Four days later he died, at the age of 47. It was a crushing blow for Friends who were already distraught over their situation. Twelve resigned from the meeting immediately, two more soon afterwards, and 42 others signed a letter of protest but chose to stay and work for change within the meeting. Joseph Bevan Braithwaite, however, wrote in his diary after Duncan's death: "How wonderful are the ways of Providence!"

The little group organized itself for worship and discussion, usually with about 35 people present. They did not give themselves a name, since it was not their intention to start a new sect. Joseph B Forster edited their journal, *The Manchester Friend*, and exchanged copies with many other Quaker publications. In it appeared material written by their own members and by like-minded people on both sides of the Atlantic. The Mancunians were surprised to hear that the Progressive Friends in America (separated from the Hicksite Philadelphia Yearly Meeting) held views similar to their own. In a letter, Lucretia Mott praised them for having "truth for authority, and not authority for truth".

Then, after two years, *The Manchester Friend* was laid down. From the beginning, the journal was described as a temporary expedient to make their story available to others and to encourage writing along these lines. They called what they were doing an experiment to show the viability of a Quaker meeting based on love that overcomes differences in experience and belief. Why did the experiment end? It may have been because of their small numbers, the death of a key leader, or the fact that many of them were still members of other meetings. Perhaps they were just tired of the struggle. In any case, after 1874 the Manchester "Free Friends", as some called them, faded from sight.

In London Yearly Meeting, reform came gradually. There was one more heresy trial and then both sides backed off. Charles Thompson and his inquisitors worked out a compromise. Hardshaw East Monthly Meeting, now supporting reform, protested the use of scripture during worship. The reformers saw that progress was being made quietly, and the old guard saw that confrontation could blow back on them. In 1884 and 1886, pamphlets appeared in London urging consideration for rationalists, and in 1887 the yearly meeting declined to endorse the Richmond Declaration of Faith. And then came the Manchester Conference in 1895 and the beginning of a new era in the Society in Britain.

It is perhaps striking that it was the moderates who brought change to the Society. It is hard to say whether having a more radical expression of views helped or hurt the effort, but revolutions require many people working in many ways. Did the moderates remember the "Free Friends"? Almost certainly so. The events had been dramatic and they were reported in the Quaker press. Some people who were involved were still alive and active in 1895, and the issues certainly were still alive. When John Wilhelm Rowntree wrote an outline for a definitive history of the Society, he included a section on the Manchester troubles. Unfortunately, Rufus Jones left that out when he wrote the book after Rowntree's early death in 1905. But he did not succeed in burying the story forever: Quaker nontheists of today are the inheritors of their tradition.

Henry Joel Cadbury: No Assurance of God or Immortality

'Philosophical studies... left me without assurance for or against God or immortality'.

In a different way and a different country, Henry Joel Cadbury showed how it was possible to be both a Quaker and a nontheist. He was born into a large Quaker family in Moorestown, New Jersey, near Philadelphia, on December 1 1883. The family had roots in England: his father was a first cousin of George Cadbury, whose home became the Woodbrooke Quaker Study Centre. The Philadelphia Cadbury family went to the orthodox side in the 1827 schism that produced two yearly meetings in that city.

Henry Cadbury went to Westtown School, Haverford College, and Harvard University where he earned degrees in 1904 and 1914. He worked as a teacher for 50 years, the last 20 as Hollis Professor of Divinity at Harvard. As a teacher, he gently asked probing questions, helping his pupils find their own views instead of teaching his. He always considered himself a student, too. Professional recognition came for his studies of the people and times behind events of the Bible and he was one of the editors of the Revised Standard Version of the New Testament. He wrote constantly. Over 150 books, book chapters, pamphlets and articles flowed from his hand.

Henry Cadbury married Lydia Caroline Brown in 1916 and they lived together for the next 58 years. A warm, outspoken woman, she was active in the Women's International League for Peace and Freedom and in the local monthly meeting. Lydia taught Bible classes but did not consider herself a mystic, preferring to do laundry, she said. Late in life she published a memoir of her life as a Quaker. Together, Lydia and Henry raised four children: Elizabeth, Christopher, Warder and Winifred.

Service was an important part of Henry Cadbury's life. He was a founder of the American Friends Service Committee, a labor of love that continued for over 50 years. In 1947 he was chosen to be one of the recipients of the Nobel Peace Prize that was awarded to the American Friends Service Committee and the Friends Service Council. As well as peace, many other causes moved him to action, such as loyalty oaths, academic freedom, racism and civil rights.

In 1912 Henry Cadbury and other young Friends began an effort to heal the separations that had persisted in American Quakerism for much of the preceding century. It took them 43 years to accomplish this. Cadbury was also a Quaker historian and although he claimed to be only an amateur he made important contributions in that area, too. His friendly manner meant that he could take radical positions without causing too much upset.

A calm person with a lively sense of humor, he also had periods of depression, sometimes as a result of overwork during wartime. There was a lot of turmoil in his busy life. He worked for peace during two world wars, tried to heal a Quaker schism, confronted public hysteria during the McCarthy era, helped retranslate the Bible, and managed the confusion of an exceedingly busy life. On October 7, 1974, in his 91st year, he died as a result of falling on the stairs while carrying his beloved wife's breakfast tray.

Before going on to specific positions Henry Cadbury took that are helpful for nontheist Quakers, one other feature of this complex man's life needs to be mentioned: he was intensely private about his personal religious experience and opinions. There were good reasons for this. He didn't want his views to interfere with the searches of others, and he wanted to prompt questions rather than give answers. Personal publicity could also hinder his efforts as an advocate for harmony. His views were likely to be misunderstood, being subtle and changing, and describing them would suggest they were important when his primary concern was action.

Henry Cadbury pointed out repeatedly that beliefs are not necessarily the cause of actions. This also applies to faith, doctrine and creed. He saw these as expressions of religious experience and he looked to the circumstances of our lives for the causes. In his own life, faith often grew from action. He suggested we preach what we practise rather than practise what we preach.

This was a controversial position because Quakers typically described belief as the source of action and the basis for Quaker unity, identity and practice. However, Henry Cadbury saw that good lives are accompanied by many different religious beliefs and the same beliefs accompany many different actions. (For example, people of many faiths follow the Golden Rule, and people of one faith take many positions on social issues.) Knowing people's beliefs does not allow us to predict the rest of their behavior, and changing how they believe does not mean their other behavior will change.

Why did he come back to this again and again? It was what he observed in himself and others, and what he saw in the lives of early Friends. It addressed issues that divide us and provided a basis for reconciliation, and it opened a way for skeptics to participate in the Religious Society of Friends.

In place of a religion based on shared faith, Henry Cadbury offered a religion of daily life. He said the best way to advertise an ideal is to wrap it up in a person, to incarnate it. John Woolman was a favorite example of a religious personality in action, but he found a basis for this approach at an even earlier stage in Quaker history: first generation Friends behaved as they had to behave without first deriving it from general principles. That came later.

Again, Henry Cadbury knew this was controversial. For many it would be difficult to accept the possibility of religion without theology. He called this a genuine form of religion but one not often recognized. He did not present it as the only path, but as a good path and he encouraged those who were drawn to it.

He was blunt in describing theological views as dramatizations, as stories that present a religious approach. He called this the dominion of imagination over experience and compared it with poetry. Our religious views are individual creations. If we see this and accept it, we will have a way to love those with whom we disagree.

For Henry Cadbury, our words, which are the products of our particular histories, are inadequate to the task we set them. The expression we give of our experiences will be as individual as we are individual. We should each speak as we are moved to.

In his studies of the Bible, Henry Cadbury kept coming back to the lives of the people involved, to the concrete behind the abstract. He said that what is true in the Bible is there because it is true, not true because it is there.

When asked to address Pacific Yearly Meeting on the question of whether Quakers must be Christians, he suggested that Quakerism and Christianity are defined by sets of traits. We each select some traits and leave others. This need not prevent unity. He called for loyalty to method rather than to doctrine or results.

Cadbury said he sought a life of spontaneous response to passing circumstance, rather than one of following a pattern. What a simple idea! If we are well formed, we need not worry about how we will react. We can concentrate on being clear to react as way opens. All of this fits well with his desire to keep his personal views private. We can relax about our differences and get on with the loving!

An emphasis on lives rather than theologies has many implications for how we govern ourselves in the Religious Society of Friends. Cadbury praised modern Disciplines that replace collective statements of faith with writings by individual Friends. This presents the faith of Quakers without requiring that any particular expression of it be accepted by any particular person. It also leaves room to grow. He saw the Society as a dynamic institution, open to change, interacting with its environment and within itself. He wished we could return to the early days when Quaker membership was a reflection of life and character and of participation in the Quaker community, rather than agreement on doctrine.

Henry Cadbury called for outreach to all, including those skeptical of traditional religious concepts. He supported the presence among Friends of those who have not had what they consider to be mystical experiences. It was a dramatic position to take, since his brother-in-law Rufus Jones, and others, were at this very time seeking to set modern Quakerism on a foundation of mystical experience.

This approach can be extended to include nontheists, although Henry Cadbury only addressed this publicly on two occasions, as far as I know. These were in talks with his divinity students in 1936 and 1940. He never published this, but he did keep in his files the text of one talk and notes for the other. On the first occasion he wrote, "I can describe myself as no ardent theist or atheist." His notes for the other occasion contain this line: "Philosophical studies of elementary kind – left me without assurance for or against God or immortality".

I interpret this as a call for openness toward nontheists rather than a statement of a personal view. For instance, he does not tell us what sort of concept of God he is speaking of. On other issues he sometimes took different positions at different times, perhaps because his thinking had changed or because his real views were inadequately described by the statements he was making. (He once said he accepted a particular doctrinal point on Tuesdays, Thursdays and Saturdays.)

Henry Cadbury had a vision of the Society as a tapestry with many kinds of thread. Thank goodness we are not all alike! We can be obedient to our individual duty, and still behave as if we were bound by common standards of religious experience and belief. Henry Cadbury showed us a path to unity amidst diversity.

For much of his life he struggled to bring about healing within our Society. He showed that differing beliefs can be central in our lives without necessarily setting us apart. He offered this emphasis on lives rather than doctrine as a basis for reconciliation among Friends. Most of his attention went to the divisions in yearly meetings and between branches of our Society, but his approach is also useful in healing dissension in monthly meetings or families and when the conflict is within a single individual.

We will each find what we need in Henry Cadbury's writings. For the nontheist, he is a guide to being a Quaker in the absence of God; but he serves just as well for those who place God at the heart of their Quaker lives. Henry Cadbury offers each of us what we need. He focused on religious lives and avoiding religious divisions. He provided ways to be Christian and Quaker in different combinations, to be theist Quakers and nontheist Quakers together, to be open and to respect privacy. He showed how to form communities of many kinds of Friends. What a wonderful legacy!

He was not alone, but was in a tradition stretching back to the beginning with calls for doctrinal diversity by Isaac Penington, William Penn, John Bartram, John Woolman, the Free Quakers, Hannah Barnard, the Hicksites, Lucretia Mott, Progressive and Congregational Friends, and the Manchester rationalists. Other Friends of his own time who held their views privately but worked publicly to welcome rationalists were Jesse Holmes, Arthur Morgan and Morris Mitchell.

Since Henry Cadbury's time two other types of accommodation have been seen among Friends. One is to speak publicly of one's nontheist views on occasion, but to be known mainly for other aspects of one's Quaker life. A third option is to work in a sustained and open way for the acceptance of nontheists among Friends.

This did not happen during Henry Cadbury's lifetime. The positions he stood for set the occasion for what came later. He had a vision of how to build a doctrinally open Society. He did not see this as losing our Quaker identity, but as joining with others in a larger Quaker identity. He showed the way for nontheists to be Quakers, and for Quakers to become comfortable with religious diversity.

Further reading:

On Winstanley, see 'Gerrard Winstanley and the Republic of Heaven' by David Boulton (Dales Historical Monographs, Dent, Cumbria, UK, 1999) where all quotations are sourced. As quoted in the above essay, Winstanley's spelling, capitalisation and punctuation have been modernised. See also David Boulton's extended essay 'Winstanley and Friends', included in 'Real Like the Daisies or Real Like I Love You?: Essays in Radical Quakerism' (Dales Historical Monographs as above, and Quaker Universalist Group, UK, 2002) and reprinted in 'Militant Seedbeds of Early Quakerism' (Quaker Universalist Fellowship, 2005, QUF@sylvania.net and www.universalistfriends.org).

On David Duncan and the Manchester Free Friends, see: [1] Richenda C Scott, 'Authority or Experience: John Wilhelm Rowntree and the Dilemma of 19th Century British Quakerism' (Journal of the Friends' Historical Society, Spring 1960, 49(2), 75-95); [2] Elizabeth Isichei, 'Victorian Quakers' (Oxford: Oxford University Press, 1970); [3]Roger C Wilson, 'Manchester, Manchester and Manchester again' (Friends Historical Society Occasional Series No. 1. London: Friends Historical Society, 1990); [4] Thomas C Kennedy, 'British Quakerism 1860-1920: The Transformation of a Religious Community' (Oxford: Oxford University Press, 2001); and [5] Geoffrey Cantor, 'Quakers, Jews, and Science: Religious Responses to Modernity and the Sciences in Britain, 1650-1900' (Oxford: Oxford University Press, 2005).

On Henry Joel Cadbury, see Margaret Hope Bacon's biography, 'Let This Life Speak: The Legacy of Henry Joel Cadbury' (Philadelphia: University of Pennsylvania, 1987), and her pamphlet, 'Henry J Cadbury: Scholar, Activist, Disciple', Pamphlet #376 (Wallingford PA: Pendle Hill Publications, 2005). Also see Henry Cadbury's 'My Personal Religion' (Universalist Friends, 2000, 35: 22-31 and 36: 18).

For additional source material on this chapter visit www.nontheistfriends.org

Facts and Figures

Do Quakers Believe in God, and if They Do, What Sort of God?

David Rush

In this chapter, I will try to summarize what is known about belief in God among Quakers in the UK, and those in the US who worship in liberal, unprogrammed meetings. This question generates much heat, especially from those who are convinced that a belief in God is a prerequisite for participation in the Religious Society of Friends.

Just about every perspective on the human relationship to God, or the divine, or the spirit, can be found within the Society. To experience this diversity one need only peruse the articles and letter columns of *The Friend, Friends Journal, Quaker Theology*, or the musings in the publications of the Quaker Theology Seminar. These include many testimonies of individual liberal Quakers who are not theists (see, for instance, Rush[1], Peters' 1972 Swarthmore Lecture "Reason, Morality and Religion"[2], and publications of the Quaker Universalist Group in Britain[3] and Quaker Universalist Fellowship in the US[4]). However, there is not much information on how common belief in God is among Quakers in general. While the writings of early leaders of the Society may represent normative belief in the 17th century, the statements made in contemporary Quaker publications give some sense of how a few individual Quakers think about their religion, but there remains much uncertainty how well these individual statements represent the Society as a whole.

Surveys of Quaker belief

Fortunately, there are a few relevant surveys. The key ones in Britain are by Dandelion, done in 1989-90, and published in 1996[5], and the recently completed replication and extension of this survey by Rutherford and Dandelion[6], presented in a workshop at Woodbrooke Quaker Study Centre in November 2005. There is one survey done in the US, at ten Meetings in Philadelphia Yearly Meeting, around 2002-3, which asked questions similar to those asked in Britain[7]. Three surveys are very few, but the results turn out to be congruent enough to allow some cautious generalizations about the diversity of contemporary Quaker belief.

(i) Britain

While Dandelion's survey was done in 1989 and the modified survey by Rutherford and Dandelion in 2003, the results of the two surveys are similar, in spite of very different sampling strategies and a lapse of 14 years. The earlier investigation included shorter surveys among several other religious groups, the results of which allow us to contrast Quakers' beliefs with those of other British religious sects. In Table 1 (see tables at end of chapter) I compare the responses of four groups - Quakers, Anglicans, Roman Catholics, and Jehovah's Witnesses - to the question "Do you believe in God?"

While about a quarter of Quakers answered no or "not sure," essentially everyone in the other three groups answered yes. We can conclude that, among the participants in this set of studies, only Quakers were uncertain about the existence of God. Further, amongst Quakers who did respond that they believed in God, their conception of the meaning of this belief was remarkably different from that of the other groups (Table 2).

A third of believing Quakers think of God as unknowable, many more than among the other groups. Only a minority of Quakers found God all-knowing (36%) or all-powerful (19%), or capable of a personal relationship with the worshipper (31%), in marked contrast to the other three denominations. Thus, a simple question about belief in God, without further amplification and elaboration, could give a false impression that Quakers meant by God what others meant. Apparently, often they do not.

The attitudes of Quakers about Jesus were markedly different from the other three denominations (Table 3). The vast majority of those in other sects agreed that Jesus was "Christ, the son of God". Only 14 % of Quakers had this view of Jesus. For Friends, Jesus was followed primarily as an ethical and spiritual teacher, and most Quakers found Jesus contained "that of God, as we all do," while for the other respondents he was God, and distinct from humanity.

The results of Rutherford and Dandelion's 2003 survey[6] have not yet been published, but were presented in preliminary form in a workshop at the Woodbrooke Quaker Study Centre in November 2005. I am indebted to the investigators for allowing me to present some of these important findings, and for access to some of their raw data. While most of the questions of the first survey were asked in the second, there are a few problems in comparing the two surveys. A new question was included *before* asking whether the respondent believed in God. It was "If the word 'God' is not helpful for you, do any of the following better express aspects of your spiritual awareness?" Fifty seven per cent of respondents ticked one or more of the following: "love", "truth", "connectedness", or "transcendence", terms that traditional believers would probably not accept as synonyms for God. Another 14% ticked "spirit" or "inward light", which are somewhat closer to traditional beliefs. These responses suggested that over 70% of the sample found the word "God" unhelpful. Yet, a few questions on, 74% answered yes to "Do you believe in God?" (Tables 4 & 5).

The only ways I can square these two sets of answers are that some Friends believe in God but find the word "God" unhelpful, that they are looking for alternatives in their belief in God but are not ready to reject the concept, that they did not read the questions carefully, or that they do not theologize with any consistency.

One of the striking results shown in Table 4 is that sizable and comparable numbers of Friends, whether believers in God, non-believers, or those "not sure", said they found the same terms useful in expressing their spirituality (inward light, spirit, love, truth, connectedness). These concepts thus seem to be useful whether or not the respondent said he or she was a believer. The results in Table 5 are equally striking. Self identified believers and non-believers value the same Quaker concepts (the Inward Light, the Gathered Meeting, that of God in everyone and the Peace Testimony). The only concept to which there were strongly differing responses was "The Will of God": this was very important to believers, and not at all important to non-believers.

(ii) United States

A committee of Philadelphia Yearly Meeting (PYM) did a mail survey of 552 members and attenders from ten Meetings in 2002[8]. The preliminary, but not final, results are available on the PYM website as a PowerPoint presentation[8]. The full results have not been formally published, but one of the authors (M.C.) has generously shared the questionnaires, raw data and an updated PowerPoint presentation. These results include those from the preliminary survey.

About 20 % of responders were attenders, and 20% were birthright members. Half had attended their Meetings for 15 or more years, 44% attended at least weekly, and 44% were aged 60 or older. They had far more education and much higher incomes than did Americans in general: about half had an advanced degree, compared to only 7% of the US population; 36% had household incomes over $100,000 a year, and only 18% had incomes under $40,000 a year. They were overwhelmingly liberal in political orientation, far to the left of the general population.

The incidence of those who reported "never praying" (17%) was nearly ten times that of the general population (2%). Respondents were asked whether they agreed with the following statement: "I believe in a God to whom one may pray in the expectation of receiving an answer. *By 'answer' I mean more than the subjective, psychological effect of prayer*". Only 43.7% agreed that they believed in this traditional God, versus 85% of the US population. Thirty-seven percent disagreed, and 19% ticked "no definite belief". The apparent rate of unbelief was higher than in the British surveys, but the questions were not identical, and the one used in the PYM survey did not distinguish non-theists from those who believe in a non-traditional or metaphorical God.

Respondents were asked whether they agreed with a series of statements about religious issues. In table 6 I compare their replies in light of how they answered the question on belief in God. The majority of believers (63.6%) agreed with the statement "I have had a transcendent experience where I felt myself in the presence of God". This was less common (but not absent!) among others (40.2% among non-believers, and 27.2% among those without any specific belief). Ninety-two per cent of the believers assented to the statement "For me, Meeting for Worship is a time to listen for God," which was agreed to by 65 to 73% of others. Thus, some Friends who have rejected belief in a traditional God retain the concept when asked about worship.

Three statements strongly differentiated believers from non-believers. One was "I consider myself a Christian". Over 80% of believers considered themselves Christians, versus 40% of non-believers. Another was "I am uncomfortable with Friends using Christian language such as 'Jesus, Christ' in Meeting for Worship". While only 11.8% of believers said they were uncomfortable with Christian language, 32% of nonbelievers said they were. The third was "I am attracted to Friends more for social testimonies than for religious beliefs or practices"; 41% of non-believers agreed, versus only 14% of believers.

Two statements were agreed to by a majority of Friends, whatever their beliefs. One is "It matters less what we believe than what we do in our lives," although rates were somewhat higher among non-believers (80.1%) than believers (64.3%). The majority of respondents agreed to the statement "No one can tell me what the truth is; only I can decide what the truth is for me". This echoes George Fox's query: "What canst thou say?"

These results describe a theologically very diverse community, similar in its spectrum of beliefs to those who participated in the British surveys, with a rate of non-belief in a range comparable to that in Britain.

The disaffection of US Quaker youth

Quakers are a small sect in the US and figures comparing any of their characteristics with other denominations are rare. Smith et al[9] recently published nationally representative data on religious participation by US adolescents that identified Quakers as a distinct group. Adolescent Quaker participation in religious youth programs is among the lowest of any of 24 defined denominations, and is the lowest in church attendance. Why discuss these sobering data when we are concerned with belief? One of the persistent accusations made against Quaker non-theists is that they are one of the causes (and possibly even the main cause) for ever-diminishing membership in the liberal yearly meetings of the Religious Society of Friends. The data presented in this chapter suggest that many liberal Quakers are not believers in God, and even more believe in a very different and less traditional God than do members of other, particularly Christian, sects. One of the clear conclusions of these surveys is that Quakers are far more theologically diverse (and liberal) than their publications and rhetoric often suggest. Might our youth sense that we are not fully honest about our theological diversity? Might we do better by openly acknowledging just how wide that diversity is, and by embracing it? Might our diversity draw some of these disaffected youth back to us? After all, how many sects can welcome those yearning for a religious life, but who cannot commit to what may appear to be confusing and overly constrained creedal statements?

Belief in God and religiosity in general are far more common in the US than in Britain. Tables 7 & 8 present some nationally representative data from the US and Britain that show that by any measure the US is the more religious society. While belief in God is nearly ubiquitous in the US, about a quarter of Britons did not believe in God at the time of the surveys referred to in table

7[10]. The other indices (belief in the Devil, in Hell, and in life after death) were much more common in the US. Table 8[11] presents more recent information on attendance at religious services, and on the importance of religion in the person's life. Rates are much higher in the US. Religion is much more important in the life of the average American than of the average Briton.

Discussion and conclusions

While these few surveys might seem a weak basis for generalization, their consistency, in spite of very different sampling strategies, different populations, and different questionnaires, suggests that some generalizations are warranted.

When asked, the majority of British Quakers will assent to believing in God. This is somewhat less common among a sample of American Quakers from Philadelphia Yearly Meeting, part of the unprogrammed tradition of Quaker worship, but the question asked was not the same as in the British surveys. At least a quarter of the British Quakers either say they do not believe in God, or that they don't know. Among PYM Quakers only 44% believed in a traditional God, one who responds to prayer.

Many Quakers who say they believe in God do not mean this in a traditional way. A reasonable conclusion is that when many Friends talk about God, they frequently mean something different from traditional and generally understood meanings of the term. Only a minority seems to believe that God is all-powerful, is available for a personal relationship, or will directly respond to supplicant prayer. One very important gap in knowledge concerns what Quakers mean when they speak of God, quite apart from the question of belief. This writer senses that the theist/non-theist divide is far more fluid than we have supposed, and that we will find this divide often to be a false one. This certainly seemed true of the Friends who described their ideas of God in Rush's survey[1].

The differing contexts of religious belief in the US and Britain are surely important to the sense of how beleaguered the committedly theist or non-theist Quaker might feel. One might guess that those in the distinct or perceived minority in their cultures might feel more threatened: theists in Britain, non-theists in the US. It is probably important that unprogrammed meetings in the US coexist with more fundamentally Christian programmed meetings: the unprogrammed meetings may be attracting new Friends who would not feel comfortable in the more conservative branches of Quakerism. This also warrants further research.

The fragmentary data on Quaker youth in the US give pause: they are less involved in their religion than those of any other religious sect. Why are they disaffected? We need data that might help us to answer this question. We do know that Quakerism is often a refuge from other religions, and that growth of the Society comes from convincement. Perhaps the youth are more non-theistic than their elders, or at least than their elders appear to be. In almost all contemporary surveys of religion in the industrialized countries rates of belief and religious participation are lower among younger respondents.

This Quaker senses that the Religious Society of Friends might be an attractive religious home to many people who cannot and do not believe in a traditional deity, and for whom belief matters less than the leading of generous and spiritual lives, especially within a sympathetic and loving community. Might we try to better communicate that such people would be welcome in the Religious Society of Friends?

Given the Quaker commitment to seeking unity in all affairs, exemplified by how we conduct our Meetings for Business, being in the majority or minority should be operationally irrelevant. It is a fact that there are theists and there are non-theists in the Society: the actual proportions are irrelevant. We generally all use the same conceptual language. All of us are Friends, and the sooner we can accept this reality, the sooner we can continue to build loving and supportive communities.

Table 1: First British Survey[5]
Responses to the question "Do you believe in God?" (%). 692 Quakers were surveyed

	Quakers	Anglicans	Roman Catholics	Jehovah's Witnesses
Yes	74	100	100	97
No + Not Sure	26	0	0	3

Table 2: First British Survey[5]
Responses to the question "Which of the following describes God to you?" (%) (multiple responses allowed)

	Quakers	Anglicans	Roman Catholics	Jehovah's Witnesses
All-loving	56	78	92	97
All-knowing	36	66	90	93
All-powerful	19	59	82	97
Capable of personal relationship	31	50	56	90
Unknowable	35	16	18	7

Table 3: First British Survey[5]
Responses to the question "Which of the following best describes your view of Jesus?" (%) (multiple responses allowed)

	Quakers	Anglicans	Roman Catholics	Jehovah's Witnesses
Christ Saviour, sent by God to deliver us from sin	5	56	71	100
Christ the son of God	14	81	90	100
God, made human	17	56	74	66
Containing that of God, as we all do	64	6	0	4
An ethical teacher	47	25	18	14
A spiritual teacher	68	41	29	18
Christ, the inward light	25	16	16	7

Table 4: Second British Survey of Quakers[6]
Respondents were asked: "If the word 'God' is not helpful to you, do any of the following better express aspects of your spiritual awareness?". Affirmative responses were broken down according to Yes, No and Not Sure answers to the question "Do you believe in God?", where(73.5% said Yes, 7.0% No, and 19.5% Not sure)

	Yes	No	Not sure
Spirit	43.6	48.7	39.4
Inward Light	38.7	53.8	47.7
Love	37.5	59.0	49.5
Truth	25.9	46.2	39.4
Connectedness / Joining with all things	22.4	35.9	31.2
Transcendence	9.0	15.4	8.3

Table 5: Second British Survey of Quakers[6]

Having answered whether they believed in God (73.5% Yes, 7.0% No, 19.5% Not sure), respondents were asked how important certain Quaker concepts were to them. The percentages are of those who said the listed concept was "very important" or "quite important".

	Yes	No	Not sure
The Will of God	75.5	10.3	39.4
'There is one, even Christ Jesus, that can speak to your condition'	57.3	41.3	36.1
The Inward Light	66.1	69.7	81.7
There is that of God in everyone	99.0	94.6	95.3
The gathered Meeting	94.4	88.9	91.4
The peace testimony	91.5	94.3	92.3

Table 6: Philadelphia Yearly Meeting Survey[7]

Quaker respondents were asked whether they "agreed or agreed strongly" with the statement: "I believe in a God to whom one may pray in the expectation of receiving an answer. By *'answer' I mean more than the subjective, psychological effect of prayer*". (43.7% Yes, 37.0% No, 19.0% No Definite Belief). They were then asked about the following statements, and those who agreed or agreed strongly are given as percentages of the Yes, No and No Definite Belief categories.

	Yes	No	No definite belief
I consider myself a Christian	81.2	40.2	57.6
I very much want a deeper spiritual relationship with God	79.4	30.6	52.1
I have had a transcendent experience where I felt myself in the presence of God	63.6	40.2	27.2
For me, Meeting for Worship is a time to listen for God	91.6	64.6	73.2
I still sometimes feel like an outsider in my Meeting	26.8	24.3	21.4
No one can tell me what the truth is; only I can decide what truth is for me	60.0	63.7	61.2
I feel I am a "refugee" from another religious tradition	17.5	22.6	19.8
Quakerism should be encouraging diversity much more strongly	42.3	52.1	40.4
It matters less what we believe than what we do in our lives	64.3	80.1	73.0
I am attracted to Friends more for social testimonies than for religious beliefs or practices	14.9	41.1	31.3
I am uncomfortable with Friends using Christian language such as 'Jesus', 'Christ', in Meeting for Worship	11.8	32.0	21.9

Table 7: Religious belief in the US and Britain (%)[10]

Percentages of general population answering Yes, No, or Don't Know (DK) to specific belief questions in surveys in 1947, 1968 and 1975. Where there are blanks, the survey did not include a question about the listed belief.

	1947			1968			1975		
Belief in God	Yes	No	DK	Yes	No	DK	Yes	No	DK
US	94	3	3	98	2	-	94	3	3
Britain				77	11	12	76	14	10
Belief in Hell									
US				65	29	6			
Britain				23	58	19			
Belief in the Devil									
US				60	35	5			
Britain				21	60	19			
Belief in life after death									
US	68	13	19	73	19	8	69	20	11
Britain	49	27	24	38	35	27	43	35	22

Table 8: Church attendance and "importance of God" in general population of USA and Britain (%)[11]

Percentages for those saying God is "very important" are of those who gave a 10 rating when asked to rate importance from 10 down to 1

	1981		1990-91		1995-98	
	US	**Britain**	**US**	**Britain**	**US**	**Britain**
Attends religious service at least once a month	60	23	59	25	55	?
God very important in life	50	20	48	16	50	?

References:

(1) Rush, D "They Too Are Quakers: A Survey of 199 Nontheist Friends", The Woodbrooke Journal 11, 1-28, Winter 2002); also at www.universalistfriends.org/rush.html (2) Peters R S "Reason, Morality and Religion" 1972 Swarthmore Lecture - London, Friends Home Service Committee. (3) www.qug.org.uk (4) www.universalistfriends.org/index.html (5) Dandelion P "A Sociological Analysis of the Theology of Quakers: The Silent Revolution", Edwin Mellen Press, Lampeter, Wales, 1996. (6) Rutherford R & Dandelion B P, personal communication. (7) Cary M, Jeavons T and the Making New Friends Working Group: "The Survey of PYM Friends at the Dawn of the 21st Century", Philadelphia Yearly Meeting of the Religious Society of Friends, 2004. (8) www.pym.org/support-and-outreach/making-new-friends/ym-pres8 (9) Smith C, Denton M L, Faris R, Regnerus M: "Mapping American Adolescent Religious Participation", Journal for the Scientific Study of Religion, 41, 597-612, 2002. (10) Sigelman L: "Review of the Polls: Multi-Nation Surveys of Religious Beliefs", Journal for the Scientific Study of Religion, 16, 289-294, 1977. (11) Inglehart R, Baker W E: "Modernization, Cultural Change, and the Persistence of Traditional Values", American Sociological Review 65, 19-51, 2000.

David Rush *is a member of Friends Meeting at Cambridge (Massachusetts), New England Yearly Meeting. He has served on the Peace and Social Concerns, Finance, Special Sources (grants) and Membership Committees, and as co-convener of the Jewish Quaker Group. He is a retired Professor at Tufts University Medical School, and a research epidemiologist and pediatrician. He has authored over 100 journal papers and book chapters. If you have any questions, please write to david.rush@tufts.edu*

This is my Story, This is my Song ...

When this book was planned, a general invitation was issued to nontheist Friends to write briefly of their own experience within a predominantly theistic Society. The responses that follow are from Friends in the USA, Britain and New Zealand, with an age-range from 18 to 80-plus.

God: a hangover from the past

Beth Wray *is a member of Medford Monthly Meeting, Philadelphia Yearly Meeting, USA. She has served on the Worship and Ministry Committee and the Budget and Finance Committee. At one time she was her meeting's representative to the Interim Meeting of the Yearly Meeting, and was the Annual Fund representative from the Yearly Meeting.*

You are asking me to compress 79 years of "seeking" into 800 words or less - quite a challenge! My experience of being with Friends has been that the Society may hold some kind of prize for diversity of belief. Everything from evangelical Friends to nontheist Friends, and everything in between! I have always felt more aligned with unprogrammed, universalist Friends rather than Christ-centered, but have felt comfortable with and appreciative of a diversity and openness that has given me permission to do my own seeking. At the same time, I think I kept hoping to feel some sign, the "finger of God on my shoulder", that would enable me to maintain a belief in Him/Her. I think that my fundamental belief has been that what matters is how you live your life each day; your actions, not beliefs.

At a 2005 Pendle Hill seminar called "Beyond Universalism" which focused on non-theist Quakerism, I realized that I had had no experience of God, no mystical insights, no epiphanies. My concept of God was a hangover from the past. I felt like a snake shedding its skin, letting go of those old beliefs (of Christianity), and the need to search for some elusive being who didn't exist for me.

I became willing to try to be in the moment as much as possible, and to call myself a nontheist. At the same time, I am aware of a sense of loss of illusions, as well as the loss of the need to continue seeking, to "know God". Of a loss of "faith", a sense of no longer having a "safety blanket," of being alone in the universe, with no trust that there is a "higher power". It is hard to be satisfied with just "being in the moment", and difficult to sustain. Staying aware (and awake) moment to moment is not easy. But at least I feel that I am being honest with where I am in my "spiritual journey".

'The energy that was present in the beginning'

Carolyn Nicholson Terrell *is a member of Mount Holly Monthly Meeting in Philadelphia Yearly Meeting, USA.. She is a member of her local meeting's Care and Oversight, Worship and Ministry, and Nominating Committees and she works on the Pastoral Care Newsletter of the Yearly Meeting. She participated in the Religious Education Committee of the Yearly Meeting for many years and is a past clerk of the Quaker Universalist Fellowship.*

I have been surrounded by Quakerism all my life, but my life has been enriched by encounters with people of other faiths. My parents were rebelling against the strictness of their Quaker upbringings. However, we attended meeting for worship regularly. Most messages in meeting had a biblical basis and there was Bible reading every day in the Friends schools I attended.

I had an important experience when I was nine, 75 years ago. I must have been wondering about God and creation. A voice said to me, "God didn't create the world – he came along with it". I never told anyone about this and I never doubted the truth of the message. As years went by my view broadened as I realized that God "came along with" all of Creation. I believe that God is all of Creation. The energy that was present in the beginning continues. It can give guidance and grace.

I have had a few mystical experiences which showed me that I am part of all Creation. Participation in Friends General Conference Gathering workshops on the Universe Story have been very influential in my life. I have become a finder, after many years seeking. I want to find ways to articulate this finding.

Silence qualified by parables

Tim Miles is a member of Bangor Meeting, Britain Yearly Meeting, in North Wales, where he served as an elder for many years. He was Professor of Psychology at the University of Wales, Bangor, from 1963 to 1987 and is now Professor Emeritus. His specialist subject has been dyslexia, on which he has written many books and contributions to learned journals. In 2003 he was awarded the OBE for "services to those with dyslexia".

After a few years as an attender I was admitted into membership of the Society of Friends in about 1960. What particularly attracted me to the Society was, first, that it did not require its members to subscribe to creeds and, secondly, that it had a major concern for peace. This latter was particularly important to me because early in 1945 I had resigned my commission in the army on pacifist grounds.

In my student days after the war I was much influenced by the philosophical movement known as logical positivism which, in its extreme form, held that sentences about God were meaningless because they could not be verified or falsified in the same way as the truths of science or common sense. In 1959, influenced by this philosophy, I published a book entitled *Religion and the Scientific Outlook* (Allen & Unwin, 1959). In it I argued that religious language was acceptable in the modern age provided we did not understand God to be a causal agency in the literal sense. In this connection I commended the formula "silence qualified by parables". I argued that in the face of ultimate mystery there is no option but silence, but that it is perfectly proper to tell parables (or "myths" or "stories") in searching for religious truth.

Moreover one can be open to a wide variety of such parables without necessarily being committed to the view that one set of parables, and one only, is the correct one - a view which I also put forward in my pamphlet, *Towards Universalism* (Quaker Universalist Group pamphlet 7).

In my book *Speaking of God: Theism, Atheism and the Magnus Image* (Sessions, 1998) I mischievously invented a character called Magnus who was to be thought of as a "supernatural" and "non-physical" being. I then tried to spell out the absurd consequences for religion if one thinks of God in "Magnus" terms. Magnus is thought of as an invisible causal agent in a completely literal sense. Those who profess to believe in interventions by such a being are misleading themselves unless they specify how such interventions might be recognised.

Since these are my views I suppose that at a stretch you could call me a "non-theist Friend". However, I dislike labels, since I regard them as divisive, and, as far as I know, my views on God are not particularly different from those of other members of my meeting. Nor would it matter if they were, since we do not require our members to subscribe to creeds.

I certainly believe that in our business meetings it is incumbent on us to seek the will of God. However it would be absurd to take such language literally. Its function is to safeguard the sacredness of what we are doing and to remind us that it is our duty to listen and let the feeling of the meeting emerge.

There are, admittedly, a few passages in *Advices and Queries* which cannot easily be taken other than literally, for example the reference to "divine guidance" in no. 28, and I hope that in the next revision this rather antiquated language will be changed.

Finally, I think it is important to reassure those Friends who feel unhappy with the label "non-theist" that, to me at least, the issue is an intellectual technicality and in no way diminishes the commitment required of us.

'Don't ask, don't tell'

Anne Filiaci is a librarian and a free-lance writer. She is a member of Chapel Hill Friends Meeting, North Carolina, USA, an unaffiliated meeting, and has served on the Publications and Records, Library, Adult Religious Education, and Scholarship Funds Committees. She has also worked with sub-committees to formulate a nonviolent response to terrorism and has co-published her meeting's newsletter.

As a Roman Catholic child in the 1950s I attended the traditional Latin Mass. There, surrounded by flickering candles, the scent of incense and the calm, soothing sound of Gregorian chant, I was transported to a place of bliss. My journey was reinforced by the endless repetition of memorized phrases in a language no longer spoken in daily life. I felt close to and in awe of a large breathlessness I could not get my arms around. This awesome breathlessness was my "God".

As a teen I left Catholicism, disagreeing with the Church about sex, gender, war and hierarchy. I never looked back. I no longer had "the gift of faith," a "gift" that would allow me to bow my head and accept the superior wisdom of others. When I went to university and to graduate school, I preferred to rely on evidence instead of faith, and sought the discipline of analysis over that of acquiescence. I became more radical in my social and political beliefs, and could not reconcile the authoritarian god of my childhood with my belief in democracy. I would never call myself a committed atheist - I didn't see any evidence of a deity, and in short I didn't really care. It's just not all that relevant to my life.

Later, as I tried to raise a child, I realized that the values I supported and was trying to transmit – values I now name simplicity, peace, integrity, community and equality – were not mores that one generally encounters while watching television or taking a trip to the local mall. I sought a community that would reinforce these values, place them within a cultural and social context. The Society of Friends was one of the few religions where I felt intellectually, politically and socially comfortable, and I came to Friends hoping to find an ethical haven where my son could learn to become a responsible and caring adult.

I did not seek spirituality in those days, and did not enter into discussions about god or theology. I worshipped with Friends in my god-free realm. No one demanded that I place my faith in a Higher Power. It seemed to be a "don't ask, don't tell" situation, and I was just happy that no one asked - that I didn't have to tell.

Later, I found that worshipping with Friends would often return me to that spiritual – albeit now godless – place of my childhood bliss – the transcendence, the ability to disconnect from self and become one with the whole. The beloved incense and Gregorian chants are missing, but Meeting is now the place where I can enter into an ethereal transcendence.

With the Friends I have found my own "gift". It is not the gift of faith, but a practice of peace and service and the spiritual wholeness that comes from mindfulness, from looking within, from an appreciation of every living moment and from my connection with others. I find this gift to be unconnected to the concept of deity. It is, frankly, more than enough in and of itself.

'Life permeating the cosmos'

David B Lawrence of Cardiff Preparative Meeting, South Wales Monthly Meeting, Britain Yearly Meeting, has been assistant clerk of his local meeting and on its Property and Finance Committee. He is currently the meeting librarian.

As children, my sister and I were sent to a Congregational chapel because in the 1960s Sunday school was deemed to be a good thing and the neighbour's teenager was willing to take us. My parents rarely attended church (though my mother nowadays takes an interest in Spiritualism, my sister in Judaism). I had one close friend at school who barely mentioned his family's Quakerism, and also a sympathetic teacher who I later discovered to be a Quaker. At school I liked reading about other religions and this led me to question Christianity. In doing Art I studied anthropological texts about shamanism that led me to believe that religion is an essential human activity. My conclusion was that elaborate religions are essentially doctrinaire accretions upon their original sources, which are those experiences that give rise to our spiritual understanding.

This casual slow pace of my religious development would have continued thus had it not been for the sudden emergence of cyclothymia when I was 19. This illness can be described as non-psychotic manic-depression, in which I experienced states of prolonged nervous arousal and hence physical exhaustion (before I was finally properly diagnosed and medicated at 36) and in which I experienced some of the classical visions described by shamans the world over. The important conclusion that I drew from these experiences was that every idea has some emotional content, and that I had been brought up denying this. This had resulted in a severe loss of self-confidence and a breakdown as I steadily pulled apart every part of my psyche to hold its contents up for critical examination without any external referent values to work from. I urgently needed a religion.

Aged 22 I learned about Quakerism in a serendipitous way and decided to try attending a meeting. I felt immediately at home - emotionally, socially and intellectually. I had been looking for a group of people to give me personal feedback, who held the kind of high moral and ethical values that I wanted to remain loyal to but was feeling cynically coerced to abandon by conventional society. I wanted to have a spiritual life and a social life as well. I had tried other groups that advertised themselves more, but I found them to be based mostly on some kind of authoritarian structure that refused to have its pronouncements critically examined. In Quakerism I found the individual space for the questioning and doubting that I deem to be a necessary part of good religious practice, whilst in the non-authoritarian "scriptures" such as *Faith And Practice* I found the necessary guidance towards understanding the shared morals and ethics of the Quaker religious community.

I had problems in applying for membership over my scruples about how to hold "beliefs", as tools to be used for a job and then laid aside. Eventually at 30 I felt that I could no longer deny my Quaker identity, and the visitors who examined me decided that I was an agnostic and recommended me for membership. Later I discovered what the proper word is for my preferred core belief and declared myself a hylozoist★ - one who thinks that life/consciousness permeates everything in the cosmos. It is that which we resonate with in a Quaker meeting, which moves us to give ministry. The closest that I have come to believing in God in recent years is in seeing this life-filled cosmos as being governed by the "Nomos" - the "Law" - of the universe which Quakerism strives to give expression to in its various writings. Anne Conway, the Quakeress Platonist, expressed similar ideas in the 17th century, so these ideas can be regarded as natural to Quakerism.

In the wider nontheist debate I see philosophical nonrealism as a postmodernist stance. I disagree with that. Mine is a realist and thus a modernist stance, and so I am planted firmly in the tradition of atheism. I call myself a Quaker Atheist, enjoying the polemical challenge and thereby showing just how important religion is!

★*The Oxford Universal Dictionary (1963) defines hylozoism, first used in 1678, as "the theory that matter has life or that life is merely a property of matter". The Shorter Oxford English Dictionary does not include hylozoism but defines hylotheism as"the doctrine that God and matter are identical".* - Editor.

Giving up the struggle to believe

Joanna Dales is a member of Roundhay Preparative Meeting in Leeds, England. She represents Leeds Monthly Meeting at Meeting for Sufferings (the business meeting for Britain Yearly Meeting), acts as Librarian for Roundhay Meeting, and is a Quaker Chaplain at the two Leeds universities.

My mother grew up in the embrace of Emmanuel Church in Cambridge, where her father was Minister and also unofficial Congregational Chaplain to the University. When she was at Girton College she naturally became President of the Congregational Society. When I joined Congsoc thirty years later they still used as their logo a green parrot, originally adopted because my grandfather's nickname was Polly.

Some of my earliest memories are of Emmanuel Church (howling because they wanted me to move up out of the baby class); but when I was six my father accepted an invitation to become Professor of History at the new University College of the West Indies in Jamaica. My mother found a church, and endeavoured to bring up my siblings and me in the knowledge and fear of God. At school I fell into the hands of the Presbyterians, where Miss Gartshore, our headmistress, taught "Scripture". I still remember the shame of getting only 3 out of 10 in our test on the furnishings of the Tabernacle.

At home we were not taught to understand the Bible stories literally, nor yet to be afraid of God. Hell did not figure except as a source of fun and excitement. Our parents did not object when I, with two friends, dressed up as devils and burned Miss Gartshore in effigy. God did not hold me by fear, but rather by a species of emotional blackmail: "How can you love me so little when I love you so much?" It was this kind of thing, I think, that made it psychologically necessary for me eventually to abandon belief in God.

Later came Cambridge and Congsoc. It was the early sixties, the time of *Honest to God*. How the undergraduates flocked to the Open Lectures given by members of the School of Divinity under the title "Objections to Christianity"! It was the time of rousing radical sermons at Great St. Mary's, the time when the Student Christian Movement converted en masse to the Campaign for Nuclear Disarmament. Congsoc combined childish high spirits, social conscience, simple piety and a readiness to take on the big questions that were in the air. I went with others to conduct services and lead Sunday Schools at village churches. I even took part in two "missions," where, under the aegis of a local church, we went round knocking at doors and inviting honest citizens to respond to the challenge of Christ.

When I had children I tried to do with them what my mother had done with me, but with less conviction. My elder son, uncompromisingly logical, wanted to know if the Bible was true, and would not be put off with evasions. (At the age of four he announced: "I know why you can't see God – it's because God is everywhere, and if you could see him you couldn't see anything else.") We took our sons to church till they would go no longer. I remained faithful, and even became an elder, while all the time my belief in a supernatural deity was being steadily eroded. I read Hans Küng's *Does God Exist?* and found the arguments against more exciting and convincing than those in favour. I read Antony Flew's *Darwinian Evolution*, and realised for the first time how difficult it is to reconcile evolutionary theory with theistic belief. At last, on an away-day with the church elders, it flashed on me that I could give up the struggle to believe. I had become an atheist!

I resigned my eldership and my church membership, on the whole with relief. To fill the gap I began attending Quaker meetings, revelling in the silence. I became increasingly involved, though for years I thought that my "atheism" must bar me from membership. I met the Sea of Faith Network, and derived enormous stimulus and comfort from it. At last, nine years after I began attending meetings, it seemed to me that I had become a Quaker, and should ratify this fact.

I have never had any trouble with Quakers about my unbelief, although occasionally a Friend has expressed concern on my account. Indeed, if I have a complaint it is that local Friends are not much interested! I need to go to the Universalists or the nontheists to get a hearing. I have had the chance to explain myself on two occasions in the Quaker Quest programme that we are running in Leeds, and find myself hardly more radical than many Leeds Friends.

I still find inspiration in Jesus – the story of his life, death, even resurrection, as well as in his teaching. Increasingly I find that I can attend Christian services, sing Christian hymns, without squirming. I think I am a nontheist Christian as well as a nontheist Quaker.

'Be wary of people who have *the answer*'

Jo Schlesinger is a member of Pittsburgh Monthly Meeting in Lake Erie Yearly Meeting, USA. She has been a convener or member of the Clearness and Care Committee, Membership Committee, Peace and Social Concerns Subcommittee, and Newsletter Committee. She also participates in a Spirituality Group that has been meeting since 2001, and has been the Program Director for a Community Outreach Drug and Alcohol Prevention Program in the University of Pittsburgh's School of Education since 1986.

How do we make sense of the world? How do we derive meaning from the chaos around us? How do we take in and organize information through our own lens to create our own reality? Can we take every experience and find meaning and lessons within it? I pose these questions as a way of considering our differences and how our experiences and perceptions shape who we are and what we believe. I was raised in a secular Jewish household. Holidays were symbolic rituals that held markers of time but not personal relevance. Early experiences significantly shaped my belief system. It was explained to me that we make our own heaven on earth, that there is nothing waiting for us; that we are responsible for creating either our own heaven or hell. My mother often cautioned me, "be wary of people who say they have *the answer*".

I wasn't sure what she meant when I was 13, but grew to understand this wisdom. When a particularly devout neighbor was particularly nasty to people in the neighborhood, she mused, "how can someone who loves God so much hate people?". All of these early messages both influenced and shaped my belief system. Both parents had a strong commitment to social justice and demonstrated it through involvement in local and international organizations. I grew to believe that one is responsible to make the world better, that actions and behaviors matter, not rhetoric, and that one is never privy to all aspects of the truth. Quaker lessons. Anne Frank's famous quote that, "I still believe, in spite of everything, that people are truly good at heart". That internal god, that sense of potential, of complexity, stayed with me. So with a strong sense of the goodness in people but without a label, I navigated through life as a nontheist.

My Jewish roots became formalities and I yearned for a community of people who had a deep capacity and respect for listening within and to others, who brought to life concepts of peace, action, compassion and care of the world. Quakers. So without a god-centered belief system, I entered into the Society of Friends and found my home.

When I discovered Quakerism, I responded most strongly to "the Light within", something I've both observed and experienced. I am not worried about the afterlife or the need for "answers". For me, science will eventually provide them all. Creativity, respect for our environment, connectedness to the world, and our great capacity to love are what makes life worthwhile.

I have found a loving community within my Meeting. The inherent quietness has given me space to find my place within it. Although strong theistic language is rare, I have come to accept and respect those who have such beliefs as not negating mine. As a Meeting we are just beginning to discuss nontheism and consider what its implications might be. I am glad to be part of its formative years.

As the fundamentalist right continues to assert its version of the truth, the more precious is Friends' diversity. I hope to find acceptance in expressing the religious or non-religious, each of us making sense of our world through our own experiences.

'I know that you will strike me dead ...'

Kitty Rush joined Friends meeting at Cambridge (Massachusetts, USA) after about fifteen years of attending. As an attender she was clerk of her meeting's Committee on Peace and Social Concerns, and is currently a member of Ministry and Counsel. With her husband, David, and others she has led workshops at Pendle Hill (US) and Woodbrooke (UK) on Quaker nontheism.

I was brought up in a secular household. I know that each of my parents had a conventional religious upbringing, my father as a Catholic, my mother as a mainline Protestant. I am guessing that they abandoned their respective religions when they married; in my child's mind, this must have been either because religion was not valuable or because caring about it could pose a danger to loving relationships. Thus, I decided early on that religion was not for me.

Since I grew up in a Christian environment - going, for example, to the sort of school which opens its assemblies with the Lord's Prayer and closes them with a hymn - being a non-Christian required me to have something of an attitude. My attitude was that of an outsider, not a joiner; a resister of authority. I also, incidentally, grew to feel a specific aversion to the symbols, and, insofar as I understood it, the content of the crucifixion story.

My parents were not religious, but they were very moral. They taught morality primarily through their politics, their lives, and through how they dealt with us children: firmly, but with humor. They also conveyed to me the idea that being "good" takes work.

When I married my Jewish husband and people asked us "What will you do about the children?" we used to laugh and say that we planned to bathe them and play with them and read to them and we thought that would work out just fine. In fact, I found raising a family to be an excellent moral gymnasium in which to practise and strengthen my capacities for love, discernment and unselfishness.

When the children were grown, however, and when I was no longer part of a teaching staff, I felt somewhat adrift. I kept thinking of Pogo's dictum: "I love the human race; it's people I hate". Maybe I needed *people*, so as to labor at loving them, rather than becoming a self-righteous loner?

Later, we moved into the Friends Meeting at Cambridge neighborhood and it became easy for both of us to start dropping in. Of course, the Meeting needed us to be on committees, even to clerk some; bit by bit, we became embedded, enamored of both the *people* and their Quaker practices, especially those that involve listening. After about fifteen years we applied for membership. However, I have to say that I don't think I have "become a Quaker". I joined in the spirit of "This is who I am, and will probably continue to be. If that's OK with you, I think we have a deal". Apparently my Meeting accepted that.

Since I do feel affirmed by my Meeting, I have become a little more relaxed about "God". Once in my childhood, when I was dragged to a church by friends, I said to God, "I know that you will strike me dead for coming here, because you know I don't believe in you!". Now there is less of that terror of being hypocritical (and getting caught at it) and a greater need to address the God-idea because so many Quakers cherish it.

Still, "worship" does not, for me, require a God-object: I go into it as into a stream - maybe a public bath, because one definitely needs others in the meeting space - where my perspectives, anxieties, and desires can be floated away, possibly to be replaced by something deeper and better. Similarly, Meeting for Business is a venue for trying to sense the desires of others, and what would be best for us as a community. But seeing that the God-idea works brilliantly for some, sustaining and supporting them in lives of great beauty and integrity, I'm happy to encourage it in you, provided you don't assert that it must be true for me.

Because, for me, neither God the rule-maker, nor God the rushing wind, nor that domesticated god of whom so many good people speak familiarly, is something I experience. My own image of god is, more and more, the God of Job. He can't be held to account in human terms - and I suspect that he has few terms by which we can be held accountable. But his *difference*, what author James Carroll calls his "radical otherness," inspires wonder. Do I think of this god as planning my journey? Never! But I see him as an enduring corrective to the idea that my own plans are wise, or important, or likely to be fulfilled, or that my field of vision is all there is.

'What matters is how we behave: all the rest is optional'

Miriam Branson is a member of Dudley Meeting in Warwickshire Monthly Meeting, Britain Yearly Meeting. She is co-clerk of Dudley and a member of Quaker Peace and Social Witness Central Committee which provides oversight on behalf of BYM.

When I became a Quaker in the 1980s no-one spoke to me about theology, except to ask whether I regarded myself as a humble learner in the school of Christ. As I regarded Christ as a revolutionary of his day, that was OK.

What had drawn me to Quakers was the way of life and the emphasis on living life as a whole, not just going to church on a Sunday and forgetting it for the rest of the week. Like many Friends, I am a refugee from another church, having been brought up as an Anglican, and having attended a church school. Those beliefs seemed totally at odds with rationality and the ideals impossible to live up to, and many people made no effort to do so. I felt an immense relief when the thought occurred to me that I did not have to believe in God.

However, during my early years as a Quaker, I accepted the idea that there was some kind of God, although I felt free to define this entity as I wished.

Later my previous agnostic ideas began to return; mention of the supernatural made me acutely uncomfortable. Any experiences I have had which could be called Good have been mediated to me through human beings. Similarly some bad experiences. We have immense capacities to behave in ways which embody some of the most significant religious doctrines and I think this is where I am now: what matters is how we behave, all the rest is optional.

My present meeting is very small and flexible; we know each other well and tolerate open discussion, so I feel comfortable there and since the recent nontheist conference at Woodbrooke I have gained confidence to speak out rather more, although I do not make an issue of being nontheist.

Cold-shouldered by Quaker silence

Gudde (Gudrun) Moller *is a member of Waikato/Hauraki Monthly Meeting, which is part of Aotearoa/New Zealand Yearly Meeting. She has held positions in her local meeting as assistant clerk and treasurer, and on the Elders and Oversight Committee and Nominations Committee.*

Some human spirits are restless while others prefer the security and comfort of certainty. I belong in the first category. From my teens I have never felt nurtured by traditional Christian theology. It makes no sense to me. Nevertheless I could never leave the idea of God alone and I have spent the majority of my 82 years searching for the meaning behind the big mystery called life.

While I have had moments of confusion, doubt and guilt I felt increasingly angry at the church. I tried to find answers in psychology, philosophy, meditation and the Human Potential Movement and was given a great deal of help from the latter. Religion should be approached in the same manner scientists use: question everything that can be questioned until we discover that which cannot be doubted. In science and religion the setting free of imagination and thought is equally necessary.

Seventeen years ago I joined a Quaker meeting, hoping that lack of dogma and creed and especially openness to new light would meet my need for discussion on spiritual matters. However, it took years before this happened.

Any attempt of mine in that direction was met with, not exactly animosity, more like a "cold shoulder", or that dreadful, powerful Quaker response, silence. Not until I took part in a spiritual nurture course a few years ago was there a chance to share my feelings about my main concern, Quaker terminology.

I identify myself as a humanist, agnostic Quaker rather than a nontheist. This leaves me open to new ideas. Fox's 17th century terminology and phrases are no longer viable and don't allow us to communicate what is of ultimate importance. As Rex Ambler writes in *The End of Words*: "We allow Fox and co the authority over our present way of thinking, and by doing that we are negating the very principle that Fox stood for, the priority of one's own spiritual leadings."

God is for me a metaphor for the big mystery of life. I don't have any particular belief, but hope and trust that everything will be well; that the mystical, transforming power that I feel resides in us is strong enough to make a better world. I see this power as being wholly human, although mystical; the depth dimension of being human. It's our potential for growth, for becoming whole, that aspect of our psyche which is responsive to spiritual values. Could we describe this inner power as a strong conscience paired with an intuitive knowledge stored in our DNA, or as a higher consciousness latent in us, waiting to be used? I speculate if this power in us is in some way connected to a cosmic intelligent force behind evolution. If everything is inter-connected and inter-dependent as the scientists tell us, then that seems possible. I am not a scientist, indeed my only higher education is the one I obtained at the university of life. I stand in awe and wonder of life with all its joys and sorrow, its highs and lows.

As our knowledge of the universe expands, so must our metaphors and language. To me life seems more and more like a process, a process of being and becoming, of maturing and evolving. True religion does not require us to believe, but to become; it's a state to be attained. As Alex Wildwood says in *A Faith of Our Own*: "If humankind is evolving slowly but surely beyond a sense of God as external, supernatural and invasive, an omnipotent parent figure, then we need to ask, not WHO God is, but WHAT God is. We have to learn to sing a new song in a strange land". Wildwood also suggests "that we must consider ways of celebrating our connection to the Earth in some kind of artistic, creative expression, something that is life-loving and reminds us that we are born blessed and holy, but at the same time does not set itself against rationality or the findings of science". To this I would add, that science enhances our sense of awe and wonder, as can the arts in all their many different expressions. We need something that can boost our faith in our own potentiality and we also need a new attitude towards the world which must start with reverence. From that will follow the values of responsibility, frugality and justice. However, we cannot think new thoughts until we are free to do so, and we cannot achieve anything until we first admit that we do not know.

'God was on trial - and the verdict was Guilty'

Hubert J Morel-Seytoux is a member of Palo Alto Friends Meeting of Pacific Yearly Meeting, USA. He is on the Library, Building and Grounds, and Nominating Committees and in the past has served on the Worship and Ministry, Oversight, Peace and Social Action, and Adult Education Committees (as clerk of the last two). He is his meeting's liaison with Friends Committee on National Legislation and the Santa Clara Council of Churches. At Pacific Yearly Meeting he serves on the Peace and Social Order Committee and is the Convener of the Yearly Meeting representatives to the annual meeting of Friends Committee on National Legislation.

It is often said that we are seekers. Rather, I feel that we are discoverers. Life teaches us even when we are not striving to study.

I was born into a French Catholic family. At a young age I went through catechism, "solemn" communion, confirmation, etc., before I had a chance to develop the self-confidence to challenge what was presented to me as "truth". One circumstance helped trigger my incredulity. When I was about 14 I read Anatole France's *The Isle of the Penguins*. It was a humorous and stinging satire on the church and its "fairy tales". It opened my eyes. Only later did I discover that it was on the "Index" [of prohibited books]. By reading it I had committed a mortal sin! My faith in the church had been badly shaken, but maybe not yet my faith in God.

While in engineering school in Paris, once a week I would read to blind men pursuing their university studies at the Braille School. We would read plays that we then went to a theater to "see". I remember vividly leading the men, who held each other's hands in a chain, between rows of colorful seats in the theater, up to the balcony where the seats were cheaper. While I led this procession, I felt myself burdened with an enormous sense of absurdity and futility. At the time I was reading books by Camus which were like spotlights for my journey to lucidity. No grandiose principle could justify the fate of those young men. God was on trial and the verdict was guilty. The Absurd struck me smack in the face, and there would be no return. I was "L'homme révolté" and would leave the sacred world of grace for the secular world of reason, albeit with severe limits. Once the question of "Why we live" has been deemed irrelevant, that of "How to live" becomes more important as well as more difficult, because there is no sacred answer any more.

In California I met my wife and she introduced me to Quakerism. The faith appealed to me because it rejected hierarchy, idolatrous belief in the Bible, etc.. However, the peace testimony kept me from joining the Society for about thirty years as the German occupation in France had left a bitter impression. Eventually revelation came to me and I became a member. I remember little of the conversation during the meeting with the clearness committee for membership except for two things. To the best of my recollection there was no discussion about God, or my belief in it. There was this gem from a wonderful woman: "We do not promise anything". It was clear that my nontheist philosophy was not an impediment.

For Quakers, as important as the peace testimony is the testimony of integrity. If you do not believe in God, do not hesitate to say so. Come out of the closet. That in itself is your honest contribution to the Meeting. In fact, do Quakers believe in God? Quakers have no creed.

A misconception is to think that, because you do not believe in God, you are not religious. By nature one is religious because one wonders about the human condition. Man is faced with the mystery of the universe and the anxiety of a final death. He knows that he will never understand the one nor accept the other. I am pretty sure that Quakers do not pretend to know either but they have a beautiful expression to gift-wrap that ignorance: "that of God in everyone". The wisdom of Quakers is that they do not elaborate about the precise content of that statement but leave to each individual the task of creating its meaning. For some, of course, it is a statement of fact. For me it is a most fruitful concept that explains everything and nothing, but whose consequences are magnificent, as all testimonies derive from it.

Community is another testimony. Whether you believe in God or not, you are part of a community: you share in warm human friendship. Indeed, specially for a nontheist Quaker, friendship is the one virtue that renders our human condition bearable in an incomprehensible world. It is quite significant that this essential value is imbedded in the name of the Society.

Search for meaning

Jeanne Warren became a regular attender at Oxford Meeting, England, after moving there in 1980, and subsequently joined Witney Monthly Meeting (Britain Yearly Meeting). She was active on the Children's Committee when her own children were growing up and has also served on the Nominations Committee and as monthly meeting representative on Quaker Life (formerly Quaker Home Service) Representative Council.

I think I was naturally religious as a child, but not spiritual or mystical. I grew up in the American Midwest in the middle of the 20th century. It was a practical, pragmatic culture but also quite puritanical. The only outlet for feeling was music, especially church music. In the liberal Methodist Church where I was raised, the things that caught my imagination were the gospel stories from Sunday School and the hymns from the church service. My parents always chose ministers with a strong social conscience, and I heard sermons about kindness and honesty in family relationships and business dealings, as well as larger issues such as racism, temperance and peace.

So my view of Christianity and therefore of religion was very much an ethical one. During my teenage years, I began to question the foundations of my religious belief, and gradually the whole structure crumbled. The problem, as I saw it then, was "does God exist?". And if not, then what is the meaning of life and what is the foundation of morality? These problems continued and deepened all through my years at college. It was like having a continual headache.

I attended Earlham College in Richmond, Indiana, a Quaker college which, in the 1950s, had about 800 students and was not well-known. I had chosen it partly because I was interested in Quakers. Apart from my courses, I discovered certain helpful books. One was William James's *The Varieties of Religious Experience*. Another was Thomas Kelly's *Testament of Devotion*. Both talked about experience rather than theory. As a French major I read Sartre and Camus. This was my first introduction to Existentialist thought. However none of this answered my question about the meaning of life and the existence of God.

One experience from my final years I remember, though I would not then or later have called it a religious experience. On a very cold winter night as I was walking back to the dormitory from the library, I recalled a notice on one of the bulletin boards about a collection to send blankets to China. It came to me that it was important that people not be left unprotected against the cold. In some strange way this was a foundation stone for me, as if I had touched bottom and could start to build. It was the only one I had for years and I didn't really know what to make of it. On the few occasions that I told people about it, it was received dismissively.

A few years later I married my first husband, who introduced me to many thinkers, including Paul Tillich and various Existentialist philosophers. For a decade I considered myself an agnostic religious existentialist. Though I continued to attend church or meeting frequently, I was stuck. We emigrated to Australia, then to England, then after our marriage ended I spent 18 months working in Sweden.

I was about to give up on my religious quest but decided first to go and study at Pendle Hill Quaker Study Center near Philadelphia. It was there that I came across the work of John Macmurray, a 20th-century British philosopher who became a Quaker. Here I found answers to my questions which satisfied me! Macmurray showed me that religion could be real. And his insight that values come from the feelings made sense of my experience on that cold, snowy night. The circumstances of that night had helped me discover how to find out what really matters. The discovery was not an intellectual one, but I needed an intellectual understanding of it, being the person that I am. Once I had that, I found that I could connect with religious language in a way that was meaningful and which I could pursue with integrity.

This marked the end of a long process. I returned to Quakers. Today, with my English Quaker husband, I take an active part in our local meeting. Many would consider me a nontheist, but it has never been a problem with other Quakers. I find the topic rarely comes up. Whenever it does I enjoy the discussion, but somehow it is not divisive. My own interpretation of traditional language works well for me, and I learn a lot from both Biblical and Quaker writings. I could never join any other Christian body because of the theology, which is bound to include something I can't believe. Thank goodness for Quakers!

God - 'the guru I do not want to worship'

Marian Kaplun Shapiro is a member of Cambridge Friends Meeting, Massachusetts, USA, and serves on the ad hoc Child Abuse Prevention and Response Committee while on leave from the Committee For Marriage And Family Life. She is an active member of the Quaker Artists and Writers group. She lives and practises as a psychologist in the Boston/Cambridge suburb of Lexington.

From the first day I sat in a Quaker Meeting, about ten years ago, I knew I was home. Unconsciously I had always honored the ideal of speaking from one's Truth, which emerged mysteriously from the wisdom of the inner world . No guru, no rabbi, no priest, no minister – but a collection of human beings sincerely seeking their individual and collective loving light. No prayers or rituals to deflect the spirit of human honesty. The belief in the ideal and the possibility of peace supported by the truly democratic and inclusive practices of the Meeting for Business.

Having been raised a secular Jew in the time of the second world war, I was unsure of how an application for membership would be received. The old warnings of anti-semitism hummed in the background. I made my application letter as straightforward as the names I use – Marian, plus Kaplun and Shapiro. My background was openly acknowledged, and I felt deep love from the members of the Membership Committee. Joyfully, I became a member.

The idea of a god, for me, is like that guru I do not want to worship. Wherever my – and your – light comes from, that light is what I have to rely on, to give and to receive. When someone speaks of behaving in ways "consistent" with the teachings of Jesus, I can feel "that person speaks my mind". However, when others speak of "following" Jesus, I feel troubled. and feel the inner press to speak my truth. I do not worship or "follow" him, or anyone. Nor can I "just trust in God" when controversial topics, such as the prevention of the sexual abuse of Meeting children, are on the agenda. Feeling that inner obligation to speak, I practise what is my growing edge: to keep in mind my respect for these good people with whom I differ, remembering their light. So, taking a deep breath, I speak my differing truth from that place of acceptance. Doing that enriches me, despite my discomfort in the moment.

I say openly, in meeting, at committees, in conversation, that I do not use

"God language" and do not "pray to God," "worship God", or "trust in God" as a creator, an intervener, a source of solace. I believe in Light and Spirit, internal to every human being. In some ways I envy those who feel safer on earth because of their theistic beliefs. Many have become dear friends, there for me in my worst personal times, such as during emergency hospitalizations of my husband. They have called, sent cards, brought soup, offered to shop and cook, prayed, sang songs of comfort to me. When my post-polio problems resurface, they carry my bags, drive me home, help me prepare a professional talk by lugging books out of my bookcase onto a table I can reach without bending.

When we talk about spiritual matters, my more theist friends say that our language is different, but that they hear my soul in my poetry and in my being. On both committees on which I have served I have felt valued, serving on clearness committees, and eventually being asked to assume the position of clerk. In sum, there may be those who don't welcome me, or my godless language, but I don't know about it. I know there are nontheists who have had unpleasant experiences over the years. But I have felt widely accepted, welcomed, and appreciated as a Friend. I think it is accurate to call me a nontheist Friend. But mostly, and surely, I *am* a Friend.

We are not alone

Wilmer Stratton *is a member of Floyd Monthly Meeting in Baltimore Yearly Meeting, USA. He spent most of his professional career as a chemistry faculty member at Earlham College (Richmond, Indiana) and was a member of Clear Creek Meeting (Ohio Valley Yearly Meeting) for nearly 40 years. He grew up in New York Yearly Meeting but had strong family ties to Ohio Yearly Meeting Conservative. He has served on many Quaker committees and boards and is currently a member of the Pendle Hill Board of Trustees.*

I have been a life-long active member of the Religious Society of Friends, having been raised in a Quaker family where religion and belief in God were important. Scattered through my life I have had occasional intense experiences of sensing what I believed to be the presence of God and in the past I used prayer frequently but not regularly. Nevertheless, I am a scientist and have always felt a certain tension between my scientific understanding of the world and the concept of God. I accepted this conflict for most of my adult life, but in the last few years I have become increasingly skeptical of the existence of God and (to my surprise) this does not cause anxiety or worry. I have even begun to wonder if I should remain a Quaker, given the strong roots of Quakerism in theistic Christianity. But my ties to Quakers and Quakerism are very strong. We share basic values, life style, social testimonies, and much more.

I have wondered whether, in some sense, I am being hypocritical but I now realize that I am not alone and it has been a relief to learn of other thoughtful Quakers who find the concept of God unnecessary to their spiritual lives. My journey of searching continues, along with my desire for honesty about my beliefs. I do have a continuing belief in (and believe there is evidence for) some kind of force or essence that is outside our normal human experience. This may be what others call God. For me it is not a transcendent, all-knowing entity, but is more rooted in the unconscious connectedness between human beings. I am in awe of the great mysteries of life and the universe, but I no longer find the concept of God to be helpful in understanding the mystery.

What do I do in Meeting for Worship? Probably, like everyone, it is mixture of things. I try to focus on and "hold in the light" the other persons present. I also try to hold in the light other persons with whom I have had recent contact and, in the case of any difficult interactions, I try to understand what went wrong and what I may have done or said to cause difficulties. I find that reflecting on the things for which I am thankful comes naturally and without effort – some might call this prayer of thanksgiving. I usually find myself meditating on some of the deeper issues of my life. The experience of a "gathered Meeting" occurs occasionally and is rewarding, even exhilarating.

The universe and beyond is enough

David E Drake is a member of the Des Moines Valley Friends Meeting, Iowa, and began serving as clerk in 2005. A graduate of Harvard Divinity School, he practices psychiatry, teaches, and writes.

"I have found profit in tracing the word (worship) back to its Old English root, *weorthscipe*, meaning *worthship*. In the religious services that have meant the most to me, the leaders have held up that which is of value, that which is of worth – this very life itself, with all its beauty, mystery, and pain. Therefore, I contend that when a religious service is at its best, when each of us is given reason to pause in reverence and awe at the interdependent web of all existence of which we are a part, we are being *worshipful*, wherever we may fall on the theist-atheist continuum". (Mark Stringer, from *Intercom*, a monthly newsletter from First Unitarian Church of Des Moines, May 2002, p. 2).

Over the years I have struggled with what unites the people who call themselves Friends. It doesn't seem to be a particular religious belief as, at least in our own Meeting, you can see a wide variety of religious backgrounds and different thoughts about God, an afterlife, and who Jesus was.

After some thought and years with Friends, the commonality seems to come down to three aspects: an appreciation for silence, interest in and support of work on behalf of peace and justice, and belonging to the community of people who come as attenders or members of Meeting.

I greatly appreciated a presentation by Deb Fisch on her work in the traveling ministry with Friends General Conference. What I heard is what I have lately been practising in my own head: when you hear someone describing their own religious beliefs, or what's vitally important to them, you "translate" their words into words that relate to your own experience and view. This is not to diminish their words or thoughts, but can help to create a climate of appreciation and mutual respect.

I attempt to fashion a "factual" view of spirituality - to look at what we can know from agreed upon facts. When I hear talk about a "personal" God I think of the infinite universe, of which we are a part. "God" to me is all around us, as we are part of this never-ending scheme. It is not something I feel compelled to reach out to or communicate with. It is, instead, an awareness I reach when I can get quiet - when I focus on the present moment. For me, Friends Meeting is a place to rest, to stop, to become quiet. It is a place from where I can observe my mind and let it flow freely or just focus on my breath to become present in this moment.

Meeting is a place where I can sit in community – sharing the change in seasons, births and deaths, doubts and callings, with a group of people who have not insisted that I believe as they do. In fact, when I have shared my struggles and doubts in the silence of Meeting, I am often thanked afterwards for having done so. And, in coming from a Christian background, I am challenged by others who profess a belief in a personal God. I appreciate the diversity and respect in our own Meeting. It helps me to grow as a person and as part of our community.

A Scientist, a Skeptic, a Jew, and a Quaker

David Rush is a member of Friends Meeting at Cambridge (Massachusetts), New England Yearly Meeting. See also his essay 'Facts and Figures' on page 101.

I was born during the Depression; my immigrant parents were obsessed with economic survival, and extracting my father's family from Poland. They were only partially successful: my grandparents, and many uncles, aunts and cousins were exterminated. My father, who arrived in the US at 18, without English, became a classic American success story. He actively participated in Jewish community life, but he was skeptical of what he called "religious fanatics". He would rather be fishing than in Synagogue.

I was Bar Mitzvahed; not to be would have shamed my parents. But that seemed the end of my religious life; growing up in New York City, the only real question about belief was which flavor of Socialist I would become. My education as a scientist sealed my secular identity. I found (and find) God an answer to a question I do not have. I cannot depend on the supernatural to steward the creation. We are what we see, feel, and experience. We are our relationships to others. We are responsible.

But...

I spent a summer in Mexico in an American Friends Service Committee work camp. On occasion Kitty and I would find solace in the silence of Quaker worship, and I also sometimes sat with a Buddhist Sangha. When we started living near the Cambridge (Massachusetts) Meeting we entered the life of the Meeting, first in worship, then in committees. We were generally welcomed with great warmth, albeit tempered with some wariness by a few. For many years we have celebrated the major Jewish festivals in the Meeting House as a gift to the Meeting. In this process, we have come to learn far more about Judaism, with its parallels to Quakerism. I now am a committed Jew and a committed Quaker. We have become profoundly at home in the Meeting.

I carried out a survey of 199 non-theist Quakers as a fellow at Woodbrooke (available at www.universalistfriends.org/rush.html) because I wanted to learn whether being a nontheist was compatible with being a Friend, and I am now convinced that it is. The response, both in the US and the UK, has been generally positive, especially from many Friends who have felt emboldened to come "out of the closet". Resentment and hostility, while inevitable, has been infrequent.

I am often asked what drew me to, and keeps me in, Quakerism. (Rarely the question really means "Why don't you go away?") This has been a worthwhile challenge. My answer goes something like this: First, the concept of continuing revelation parallels the way a scientist deals with reality: all knowledge is provisional. All our ideas ("notions"), especially those we cherish most, will and must be challenged, and inevitably, modified, or overthrown. We should expect, and indeed embrace, this provisionality. Second, the concept of God in every person is very resonant for me, and akin to my humanistic conviction that every life is sacred. This is a restatement of the Quaker quest for justice and mercy (expressed, in Judaism as Tikkun Olam, the obligation to repair the world). Third, I find the commitment by Friends to lead as good lives as possible, while accepting one's all too human limitations, exhilarating. Fourth, I have found the depth of the loving relationships in our meeting allows us to go beyond belief to experience each other's deepest selves. Fifth, the daily practice of respect and civility has become a beacon in my life: listening with my whole heart and mind, trying not to interrupt, trying to achieve unity: trying not to oppress by words or deeds, especially in business meeting. Where else can one learn these skills? And, finally, there is the blessed silence...

Wholehearted acceptance as an atheist Friend

Anita Bower is a member of Nottingham Monthly Meeting of Baltimore Yearly Meeting, USA. She is, or has been, recording clerk, a Religious Education teacher, and a member of the Religious Education, Ministry and Counsel, and Nominating Committees. She also facilitates a women's worship-sharing group - and she is her meeting's unofficial gardener!

My first memory of atheism was walking home from church alone and realizing I did not believe in God. I must have been nine years old. I did not tell anyone as I was surrounded by adults who had dedicated their lives to doing God's work as Methodist missionaries.

I left organized religion a year after leaving home, disillusioned with what my uncompromising 17-year-old-standards considered hypocrisy in the church. College and young adulthood were lonely, confused and painful, reinforcing my conclusion that there was no loving God to help me.

In my late twenties I began attending a Protestant church in a search for depth and meaning. Maybe I had made a mistake in rejecting God. I read spiritual and theological books, attended church regularly, prayed and took retreats at a nurturing Benedictine priory. I discussed my doubts and questions with Christians I respected. Although I wanted to believe in God, I was unable to make the requisite leap of faith.

After several years I was no longer able to say the responsive readings or sing the hymns I did not believe. Friends invited me to a new Quaker worship group. About four of us gathered in their living room. I gratefully sank into the peace of silence. The silence was a balm to my spirit. Here I found the freedom and space in which to plumb my depths, to pursue my doubts and questions, to discover my own beliefs. I have attended Quaker Meeting since that day in 1980.

In Quakerism I hoped I could come to God without needing to make a leap of faith. Quakerism is an experiential, not a creedal religion. I thought I might experience "that of God" in meeting for worship. During the ensuing years I lived, acted and thought as if I believed in God. I was not being deceitful. I was trying to believe, to have faith, to experience God's presence.

I tried different labels for God: Inner Teacher, Light, Love, a Greater Power,

Spirit. These new names helped eliminate my childhood "Santa Clause" god, and were meaningful in focusing my meditations and reflections. However, none necessitated a belief in an active power or consciousness existing within and beyond humans, which (or who) provides guidance and strength, and deserves to be worshiped. More troubling, I did not experience something I could name God or "that of God". Yes, I had deep, meaningful experiences in and out of meeting for worship. Yes, I gained insights, felt deep love and peace, learned to be in a centered place and experienced the gathered meeting. But none of these experiences seemed to involve a Greater Power. Several years into my Quaker attendance, a weighty Friend quietly said "I don't believe in God". I never heard her say this again, but it opened up the possibility of being both an atheist and a Quaker.

As I grew in self-confidence, I allowed the doubts I had about God to emerge within me. I quit pushing them away and let them be. Eventually, I began taking them seriously. Courage was required because this was a solo journey. Most everyone I admired and loved had a deep belief in God which gave meaning and direction to their lives. Attending meeting was a weekly reminder that most Quakers believe in God. The passage of years was required for me to trust my own truth. Finally, I acknowledged to myself and to my family that God was not a reality in my life experience. I was once again an atheist.

Moving to Nottingham Monthly Meeting (Baltimore Yearly Meeting, USA) provided an opening to come out of the closet. I requested a clearness committee to consider my transfer of membership. I wanted the Meeting to accept me with full knowledge of my atheism. The clearness committee did not find my beliefs, or rather, non-beliefs, strange, and gave me their wholehearted support. My membership was approved by the Meeting. For several years I was vocal in Meeting about my atheism. Although some Friends were puzzled, I was fully accepted and never criticized for being an atheist. What a joy!

Once my atheism was in the open, I discovered like-minded Quakers. I read an article by an atheist Quaker; met an atheist woman at a Quaker Women's Retreat; participated in a survey of nontheist Friends; attended a Pendle Hill weekend and a Baltimore YM workshop on nontheism; joined the nontheist Friends email discussion list and read articles on the nontheist Friends web site.

Knowing I am not the only atheist Quaker makes calling the Society of Friends my spiritual home a less lonely and more joyful experience. I feel I belong.

A concept of goodness

Lincoln Alpern is 18 and an attender at Scarsdale Monthly Meeting, Purchase Quarterly Meeting, New York Yearly Meeting.

I am a nontheist. Though I am not a member of the Religious Society of Friends, I am a deep believer in the values of Quakerism. I would not say that I am not religious. I hold spiritual beliefs that do not center on a God figure, but rather a fundamental driving force in nature. I don't have a word for this force, but I would define it loosely as a guiding ideal that was created *with* the universe but did not *create* it. I would also define it, even more loosely, as peaceful and benevolent. When we go against these ideals of peacefulness and benevolence we go against this force of nature. It is one of those things that no human, no matter how advanced, can ever rise above. But the idea of it as an omnipotent, omniscient entity... no, that I can't believe.

One of my earliest objections to the idea of God - and the supernatural in general, for that matter, which I would define as "anything that cannot be scientifically proven or understood to some degree" - is that there *can* be no proof of the existence of either, only speculation. For whatever reason, I've grown up to be a person of certainties, and God is no certainty to me, whereas even the "uncertainty principle" is certainty of a sort.

I think the earliest important moment in my life that I can point to occurred when I was eight or nine, when my mother was removed from our Meeting and the Religious Society of Friends. I had no idea why anyone would do that to my mother, who is about as devout a Quaker as you can meet without going into borderline fanaticism. So my father explained that they had thrown her out because she didn't believe in God, and he mentioned that *he* did not believe in God either.

For some reason that incident sticks in my mind, maybe because I had never heard my parents' beliefs spelled out before. Maybe because I'd never thought about what *I* really believed before. Maybe because it was such a traumatic experience for my mom.

Another incident that comes to mind is one time a year or two before or after that, when I asked my mom what she thought God was. Her answer was that, to her, God was some idea, a concept of goodness that exists within us all. The answer stays with me to this day.

So for probably at least a decade I've held that the supernatural is mere superstition. I tend to get a little unsettled or amused when I encounter any deeply God-oriented religious stuff. Still, one strives for tolerance, always. I make no attempt to hide my nontheism, but neither do I make a point of mentioning it to everyone I meet. I think I'm sufficiently open about myself that some of the people I know well at Scarsdale Meeting know I'm a nontheist, but as far as I can tell this doesn't change how they look at me in any way. In any case, I am who I am, and I'm comfortable with that and with other people's beliefs - mostly comfortable, anyway. What other people think and feel are important, of course, and we should always attempt to take their thoughts and feelings into account, but if you are content in yourself, that certainly counts for something.

One label: just 'Quaker'

Elaine Ruscetta is a member of Atlanta Monthly Meeting in Southern Appalachian Yearly Meeting and Association. She has been the clerk of the Young Friends group of her Yearly Meeting and a co-leader of the 'Nontheism Among Friends' workshop at the 2004 Friends General Conference Gathering. She also attended the 2005 World Gathering of Young Friends in Lancaster, England.

I attended the 2004 Friends General Conference nontheist workshop, not as an adamant nontheist seeking recognition and support but as a young F/friend curious to explore all kinds of beliefs while in search of my own identity within the Religious Society of Friends. Finding one's religious identity is a lifelong and ever-changing process. However, being only 18, I feel that my views are changing very rapidly, and thus I have chosen only one label for myself for the time being: Quaker.

Despite (or perhaps because of) the fact that Quakerism as both a spiritual and practical guide has been an integral aspect of my life for most of my 18 years, I treat Quakerism as more of a philosophy and call to action than a religion. This attitude has contributed to my presence in the nontheist community although I do not necessarily identify as a nontheist. I have been gratefully educated over the last year through the nontheist email discussion list and my wonderful co-leaders of this year's workshop. I have come to admire the openness and wisdom that manifest themselves in our discussions and essays. I feel that the Society as a whole can and will benefit from this outspoken and important group of people. Quaker testimony states that every individual has a part of "God" – to me a part of "ultimate truth". Thus our call to integrity not only asks but insists that we explore the personal truths of each person we encounter. This, of course, includes the views of Quaker nontheists.

Personal religion/theology aside, I have had numerous experiences as a Quaker that I have felt to be genuine. I have been uplifted by gathering with F/friends in silence. I have been blessed with the opportunity to gather the sense of a meeting through my recent role as clerk, an experience unmatched by any other in my life. I have listened to and appreciated messages, both God-centered and otherwise, in meeting for worship. I have enjoyed six years of support and sharing in my Quaker Youth Group. I have been led to social action with the purpose of bettering our society. All these events may very well have involved some sort of God, or they might not have. What matters to me is that they happened.

Making Contact

"You may say that I'm a dreamer / But I'm not the only one" - *John Lennon*

Nontheist Friends have created a website you can visit at
www.nontheistfriends.org

The site contains news and articles by Friends and others interested in discussing Quaker nontheism, and has links to other related sites. If you are moved or stimulated by what you have read in this book, you'll find like-minded company on the site.

On **www.nontheistfriends.org** we seek to explore our own perspectives and reflect on the meaning and implications of nontheism in a Quaker context. This is also a place where Friends of all viewpoints are welcome to visit and join in a deeper conversation. All are invited to submit writings, add comments, or join the website's forum.

There is also an email list where Quaker nontheists from all over the world participate in an on-line discussion. For more details email **listinfo@nontheistfriends.org**

Many nontheist Friends are members of the non-denominational Sea of Faith Network in Britain, which welcomes all who wish "to explore and promote religious faith as a human creation". Its website is at **www.sofn.org.uk** The Network has a branch in the USA (contact Hershey Julien at **hjulien@sbcglobal.net**) and there are sister Networks in Australia (**www.sof-in-australia.org**) and New Zealand (**www.sof.wellington.net.nz**).

Email correspondence on matters arising from this book may be addressed to the editor at **davidboulton1@compuserve.com** or at the address below.

And those who don't have access to the internet but wish to connect up with the informal international fellowship of nontheist Friends are welcome to write to the editor c/o DHM, Hobsons Farm, Dent, Cumbria LA10 5RF, UK.

Also published by Dales Historical Monographs...

Dales Historical Monographs is the imprint of David and Anthea Boulton, founded in 1985, originally for the publication of research on Yorkshire Dales local history and reprints of local history classics by Adam Sedgwick and the 19th century Quaker writer Mary Howitt.

With *Early Friends in Dent: The English Revolution in a Dales Community* (David Boulton,1986) and *In Fox's Footsteps* (David and Anthea Boulton, 1998 and 2004), the imprint added Quaker history and theology. Both books are now out of print, though a reprint of *Early Friends* and a second reprint of *In Fox's Footsteps* is planned.

Still in print are:

Gerrard Winstanley and the Republic of Heaven by David Boulton, Foreword by Michael Foot, 1999, ISBN 0 9511578 4 1 (£9.00 UK, $15 USA)

Real Like the Daisies or Real Like I Love You?: Essays in Radical Quakerism by David Boulton, in association with the Quaker Universalist Group, 2002, ISBN 0 9511578 5 X (£7.50 UK, $12 USA)

The Trouble with God: Building the Republic of Heaven by David Boulton, published by O Books, an imprint of John Hunt Publishing, 2002 and 2005, ISBN 1 905047 06 1 (£11.99 UK, £24.95 USA)

Orders and enquiries to davidboulton1@compuserve.com or write to DHM, Hobsons Farm, Dent, Cumbria LA10 5RF, UK.

Godless for God's Sake is published by Dales Historical Monographs
on a non-profit basis. All revenues after recovery of costs
will be donated to Quaker projects as directed by
the nontheist Friends book group.

The Trouble with God
Building the Republic of Heaven
by David Boulton

A new revised and expanded international edition of the book described by **The Friend** as 'Iconoclastic and uplifting, but not for the theologically faint-hearted'. **The New Seeker:** 'Never less than brilliantly articulate and humorously profound'. **Universalist:** 'Engaging, witty informative ... offers entertainment, scholarship and provocation'.

Modern Believing called it 'A wonderful repository of religious understanding and a liberal theologian's delight'. **Richard Holloway found it** 'affectionate, sane, learned and extremely funny'. **New Zealand's Lloyd Geering described it as** 'disarmingly honest, beautifully written ... interprets today's confusing religious situation, spurring us on to new visions'.

Tony Benn recommended it to 'lapsed atheists ... and all who think deeply about the meaning of our existence'. **Don Cupitt said it** 'connects us with the great tradition of political and religious radicalism ... with a great gift of being funny and serious at once'.

Hailed as "a minor classic" by Robert Funk of the Westar Institute, California, 'The Trouble with God' offers one nontheist Friend's vision of a reasonable faith for the 21st century.

Published by O Books (John Hunt Ltd) at £11.99 (UK), $24.95 (USA). Available from any bookshop (quote ISBN 1 905047 06 1) or the Quaker Bookshop, Euston Road, London NW1 2BJ, UK, or Quaker Books of Friends General Conference, 1216 Arch St., Ste 2B, Philadelphia, PA 19107, USA